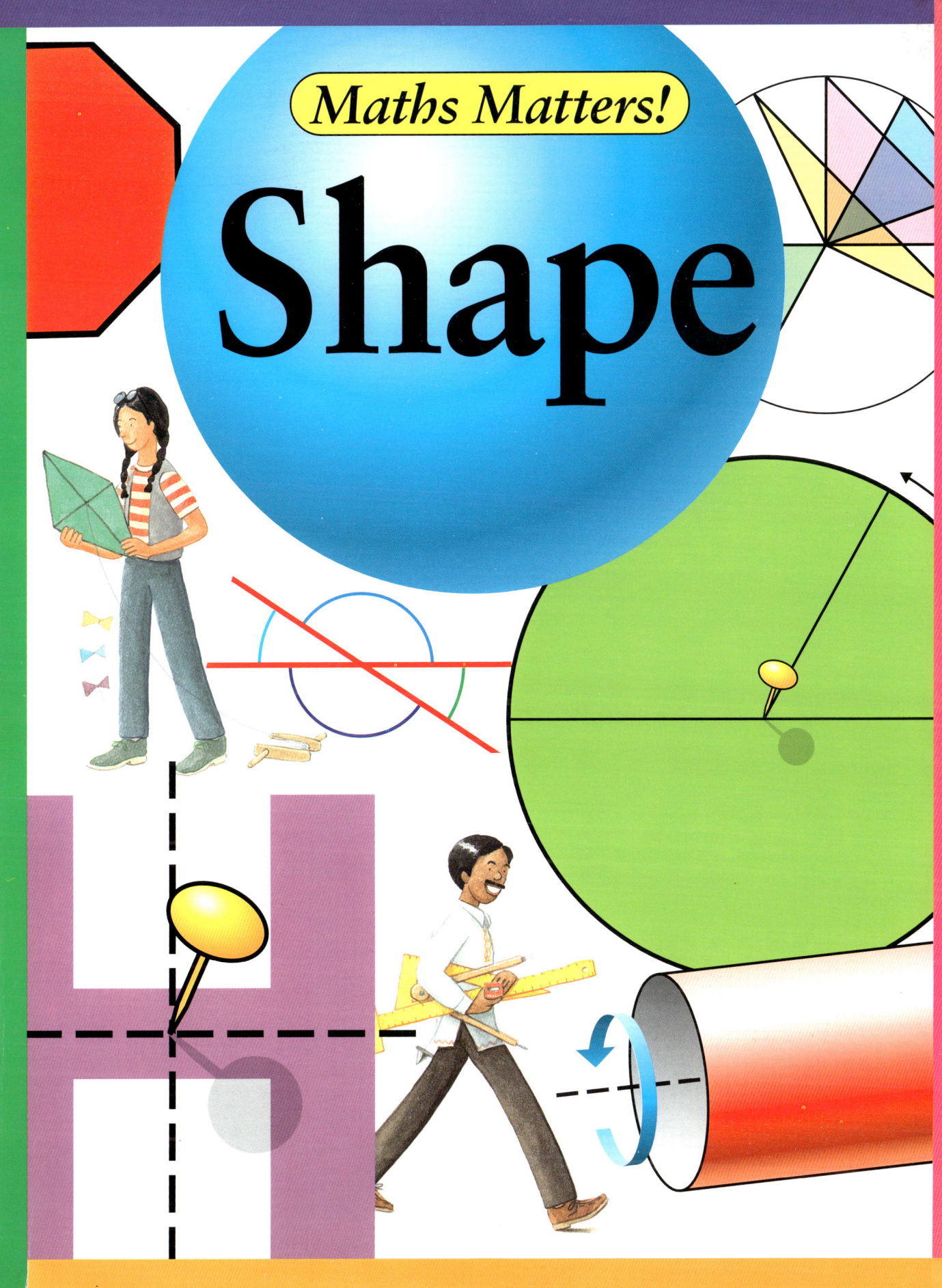
Maths Matters!
Shape

Look out for these sections to help you learn more about each topic:

Remember...
This provides a summary of the key concept(s) on each two-page entry. Use it to revise what you have learnt.

Word check
These are new and important words that help you understand the ideas presented on each two-page entry.

All of the word check entries in this book are shown in the glossary on pages 45 to 47. The versions in the glossary are sometimes more extensive explanations.

Book link...
Although this book can be used on its own, other titles in the *Maths Matters!* set may provide more information on certain topics. This section tells you which other titles to refer to.

An Atlantic Europe Publishing Book

Series concept by *Brian Knapp and Duncan McCrae*
Text contributed by *Brian Knapp and Colin Bass*
Design and production by *Duncan McCrae*
Illustrations of characters by *Nicolas Debon*
Digital illustrations by *David Woodroffe*
Other illustrations by *Peter Bull Art Studio*
Editing by *Lorna Gilbert and Barbara Carragher*
Layout by *Duncan McCrae and Mark Palmer*
Reprographics by *Global Colour*
Printed and bound by *LEGO SpA, Italy*

Copyright © 1999
Atlantic Europe Publishing Company Limited

First published in 1999 by
Atlantic Europe Publishing Company Limited,
Greys Court Farm, Greys Court,
Henley-on-Thames, Oxon, RG9 4PG, UK.

All rights reserved. No part of this publication may be reproduced, stored in a retrieval system, or transmitted in any form or by any means – electronic, mechanical, photocopying, recording or otherwise – without prior permission of the Publisher.

Suggested cataloguing location
Shape – Maths Matters! set, volume 8
  Geometrical constructions – Juvenile literature
  Knapp, Brian and Bass, Colin
  516.1'5

ISBN 1 862140 36 7

Picture credits
All photographs are from the *Earthscape Editions* photolibrary.

This book is manufactured from sustainable managed forests. For every tree cut down at least one more is planted.

The 13 volumes in the *Maths Matters!* set are:

  1 Numbers
  2 Adding
  3 Subtracting
  4 Multiplying
  5 Dividing
  6 Decimals
  7 Fractions
  8 Shape
  9 Size
10 Tables and Charts
11 Grids and Graphs
12 Chance and Average
13 Mental Arithmetic

Contents

4	Introduction
6	Angles
8	Angles add up
10	Angles that are together or opposite
12	What is a regular shape?
14	Triangles
16	Right-angled triangles
18	Triangles with equal angles
20	How to draw triangles
22	Simple symmetry and triangles
24	Many-fold turning symmetry
26	Symmetry in letters
28	Patterns of interlocking triangles
30	Quadrilaterals
32	Trapeziums
33	Kites and darts
34	Parallelograms
36	Rectangles and squares
38	Ovals and circles
40	Solid shapes
41	Pyramids
42	Cylinders and cones
43	Spheres
44	What symbols mean
45	Glossary
48	Index

Introduction

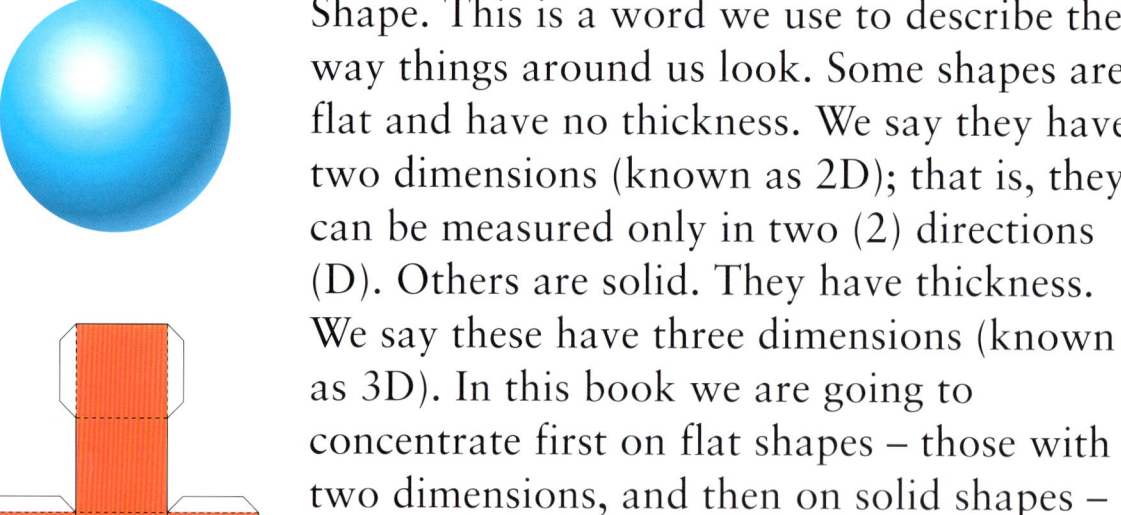

Shape. This is a word we use to describe the way things around us look. Some shapes are flat and have no thickness. We say they have two dimensions (known as 2D); that is, they can be measured only in two (2) directions (D). Others are solid. They have thickness. We say these have three dimensions (known as 3D). In this book we are going to concentrate first on flat shapes – those with two dimensions, and then on solid shapes – those with three dimensions.

Mathematicians look for precise ways of describing shapes. You will find out about them in this book.

There are many kinds of shapes, but we can start to make sense of them if we name them according to the numbers of sides they

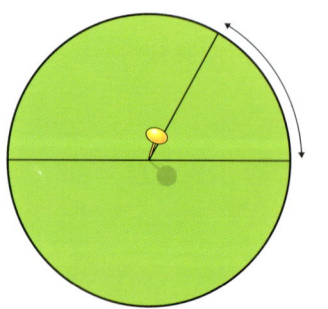
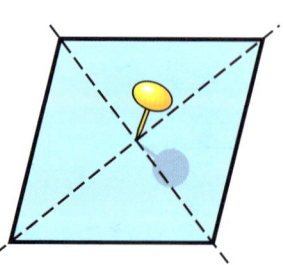

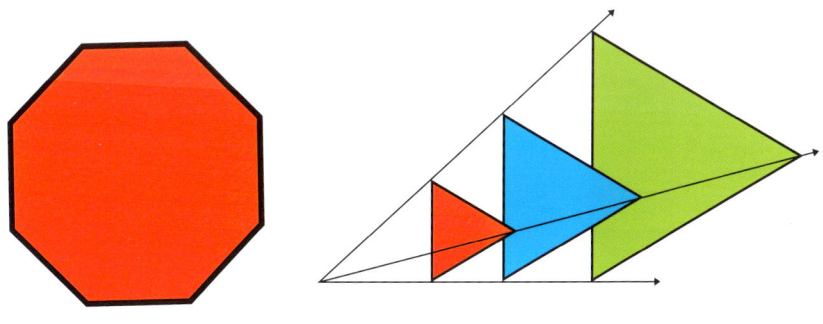

have. You will know some of these shapes already, such as a square, which has four sides, each side being the same length.

Shapes have other important properties. One of them is called symmetry. If a shape has symmetry, it can be picked up and turned around, or sometimes turned over and placed back down again so that you can't see the difference. Some shapes have more symmetry than others.

As you go through this book you will find out about the properties of a wide range of shapes. For example, you will find that many shapes fit together and interlock so that they completely cover an area.

The study of shapes is part of geometry. Enjoy finding out about some of the many shapes in the world as you read this book.

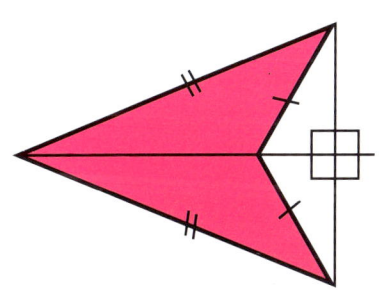

Angles

A shape has many properties. One of the most important is the angles formed where edges meet.

Angles are formed where two edges (straight lines) meet or cross. An angle is also found where two surfaces meet or cross.

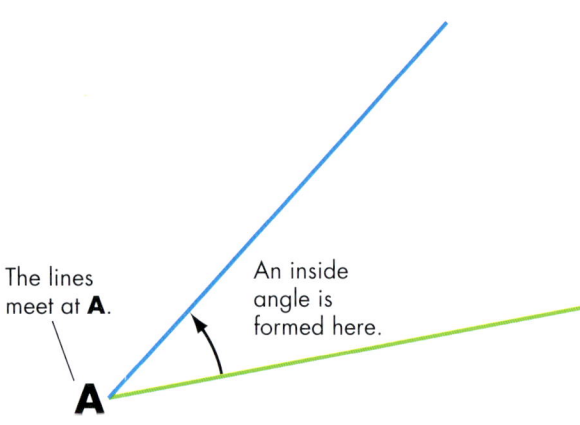

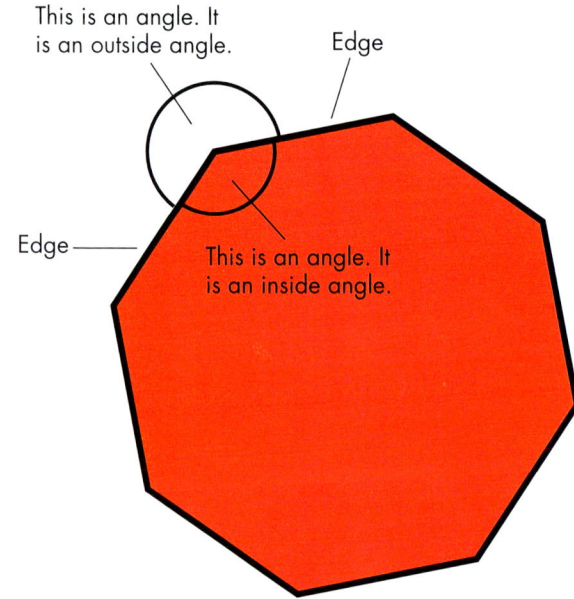

Angles are found everywhere around us. Open a door, for example, and you will see that the door makes an angle with the wall. The corners of this book have angles where the sides meet the top and bottom of the page. The corners of a table also have angles where the sides meet.

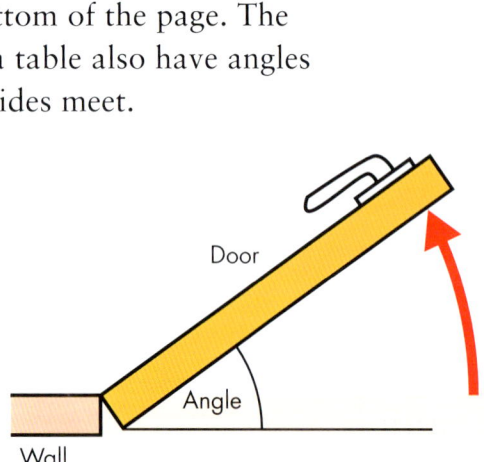

Angles and turning

One easy way to think about angles is to use your arms as though they were straight lines. If you first stand with your arms outstretched straight ahead and your hands together, then move one of your arms away from the other, an angle is formed between your arms.

Notice that you have to turn one arm to make an angle. This is why angles are often thought of as the amount of turn.

You can also get a feel for angles by turning your body. One complete turn of your whole body makes a complete circle and brings you back to where you started; in half a turn you turn back to front; and in a quarter of a turn you face to the side.

You can see how angles change as you turn the pages of a book or open a door.

Remember... It is often easier to think of angles as an amount of turn. Use your arms to help you think about angles.

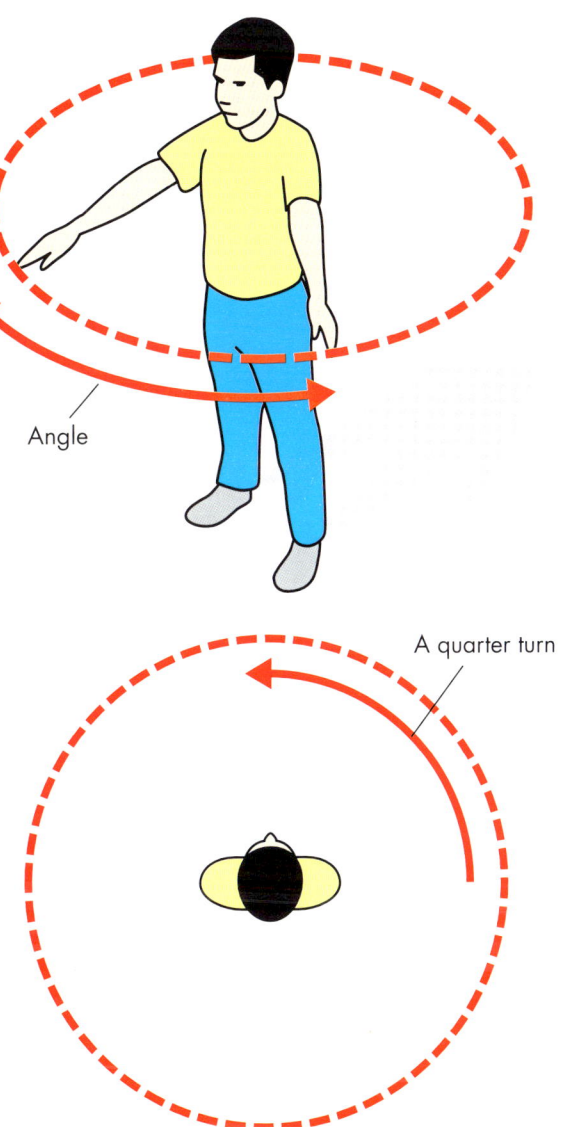

Angle

A quarter turn

Word check

Inside angle: The smaller angle between the lines at a corner.

Line: A continuous mark made on a surface. It may be straight or curved, and it can go on for ever in both directions.

Outside angle: The angle at a point measured outside the shape it belongs to.

Vertex: A point at which two lines cross or meet. Also a point at which three or more edges meet.

Book link... For more information on measuring angles see the book *Size* in the *Maths Matters!* set.

Angles add up

One of the most important things to understand is the way that angles are connected. Here you will see how to describe different kinds of angle.

An angle that we are interested in is always marked with a curved line like this.

Angles between lines make a whole turn

By drawing two lines which cross at any angle you can see that the four angles **a**, **b**, **c** and **d** make up a whole turn.

By making these four angles the same, the lines become <u>perpendicular</u> to each other. Each of the four angles is exactly one-quarter of a complete turn and so it is a <u>right angle</u>.

Right angles are marked with a special 'corner' symbol like this.

Angles on a line add up to half a turn

If you draw a ray (a straight line in one direction) away from a point on a line, you make two angles, one on either side of the ray.

If the angles are equal they are quarter turns, or right angles. Two right angles add up to a straight angle.

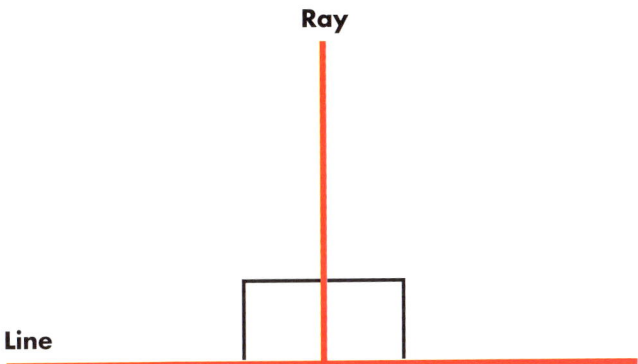

Small and large angles

When the angles on either side of a ray are not the same, one must be larger than the other. The larger angle is called an obtuse angle, and the smaller angle is called an acute angle. Acute is another word for 'sharp', and obtuse is another word for 'blunt'.

Although they are different angles, they still lie on a straight line and so they still add up to half a turn.

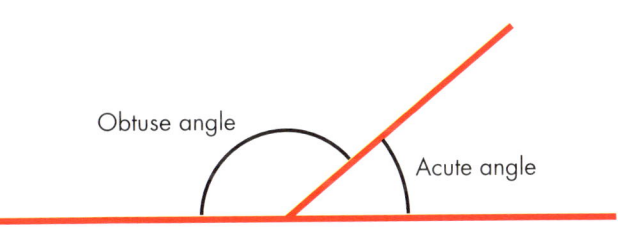

Remember... The angles where two lines cross add up to a complete turn. The angles where a ray meets a line (but does not cross) add up to half a turn or a straight angle.

Word check

Acute angle: An angle that is smaller than a right angle.

Obtuse angle: An angle which is larger than a right angle and smaller than a straight angle.

Perpendicular: Two lines which meet or cross at right angles are called perpendicular.

Ray: A straight line that starts from a point and goes straight on for ever in one direction only.

Right angle: An angle which is exactly a quarter of a complete turn.

Straight angle: An angle that is exactly half a turn.

Angles that are together or opposite

When two straight lines cross to form angles, some interesting things happen. You can find out more below.

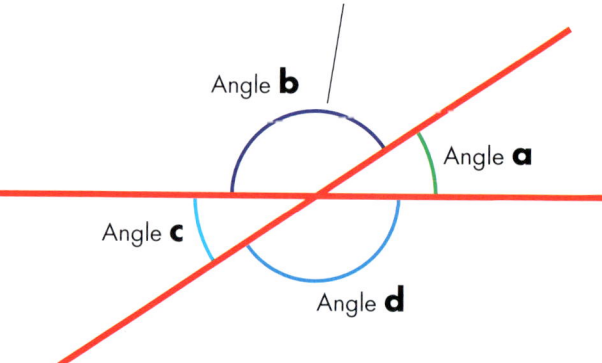

An angle that we are interested in is always marked with a curved line like this.

When straight lines cross, you have four angles. These angles have some interesting properties. The angles are marked as **a**, **b**, **c** and **d** on this diagram.

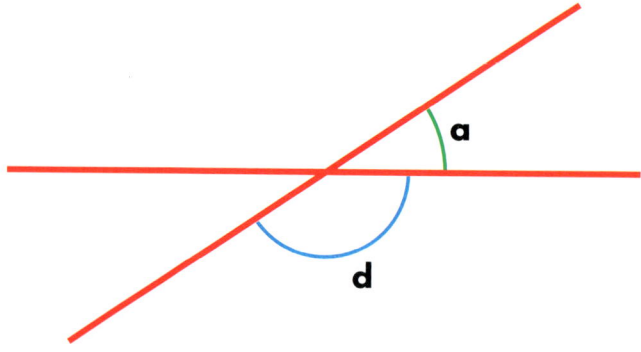

In our investigation, let's concentrate on just two of the angles to begin with. Notice that these two angles (**a** and **d**) are next to each other and add up to a straight angle, or half a turn. This is because they both lie on a straight line.

Now let's look at one of these angles (**a**) and its other neighbour (**b**). These also lie on a straight line, and so, again, they add up to half a turn.

Therefore angles **a** and **b** add up to half a turn, and so do angles **a** and **d**.

Because one of these angles (angle **a**) is the same in each case, the other two angles (**b** and **d**) must be equal in size.

This brings us to another important fact about angles: opposite angles are always the same size. Therefore angle **c** (which is opposite angle **a**) must also be equal in size to angle **a**.

Angle **a** is opposite **c** and so is equal in size. The same is true of angles **b** and **d**.

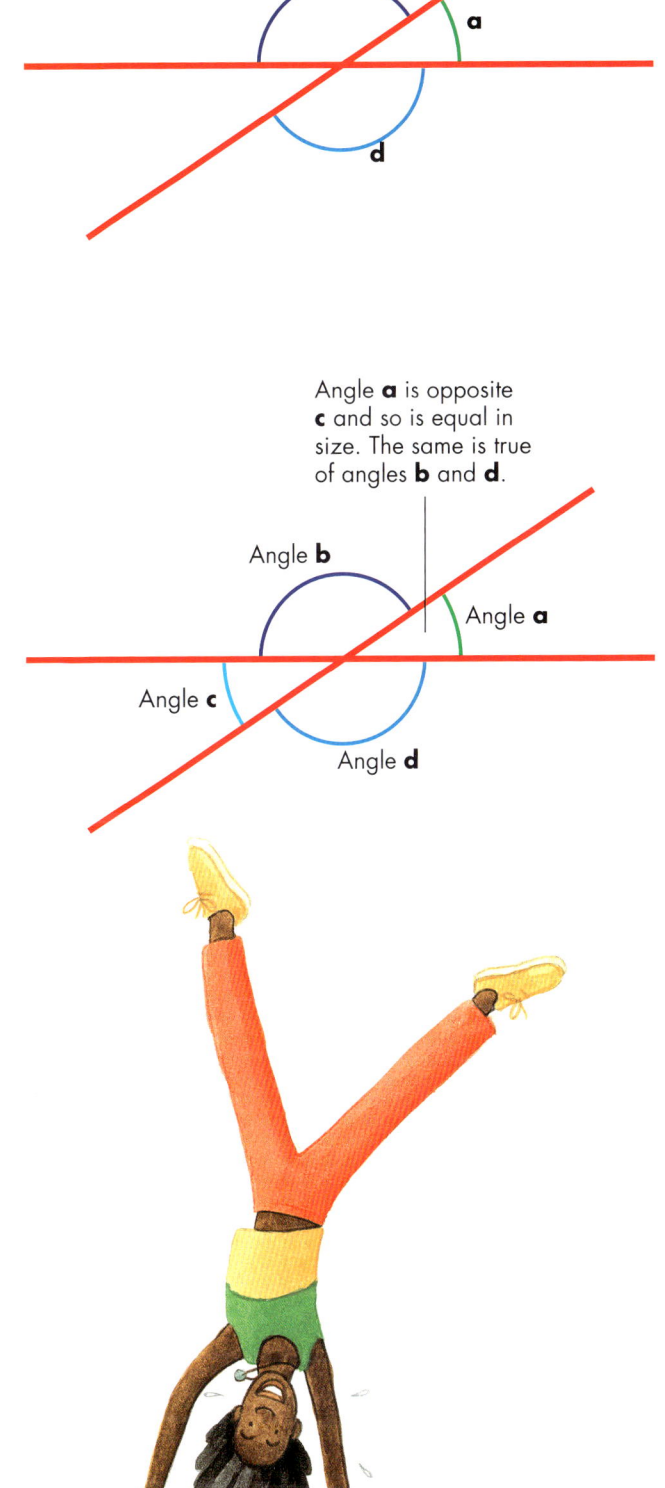

Remember... Angles on a line that are next to one another make a straight angle. Angles that are opposite are equal to one another.

11

What is a regular shape?

A regular shape must have all of its sides and all of its angles equal in size.

Regular is a special word in mathematics. Any shape with straight sides can only be called regular when all of its sides are the same length and all of its angles are the same size. All of the five shapes on the right are regular shapes.

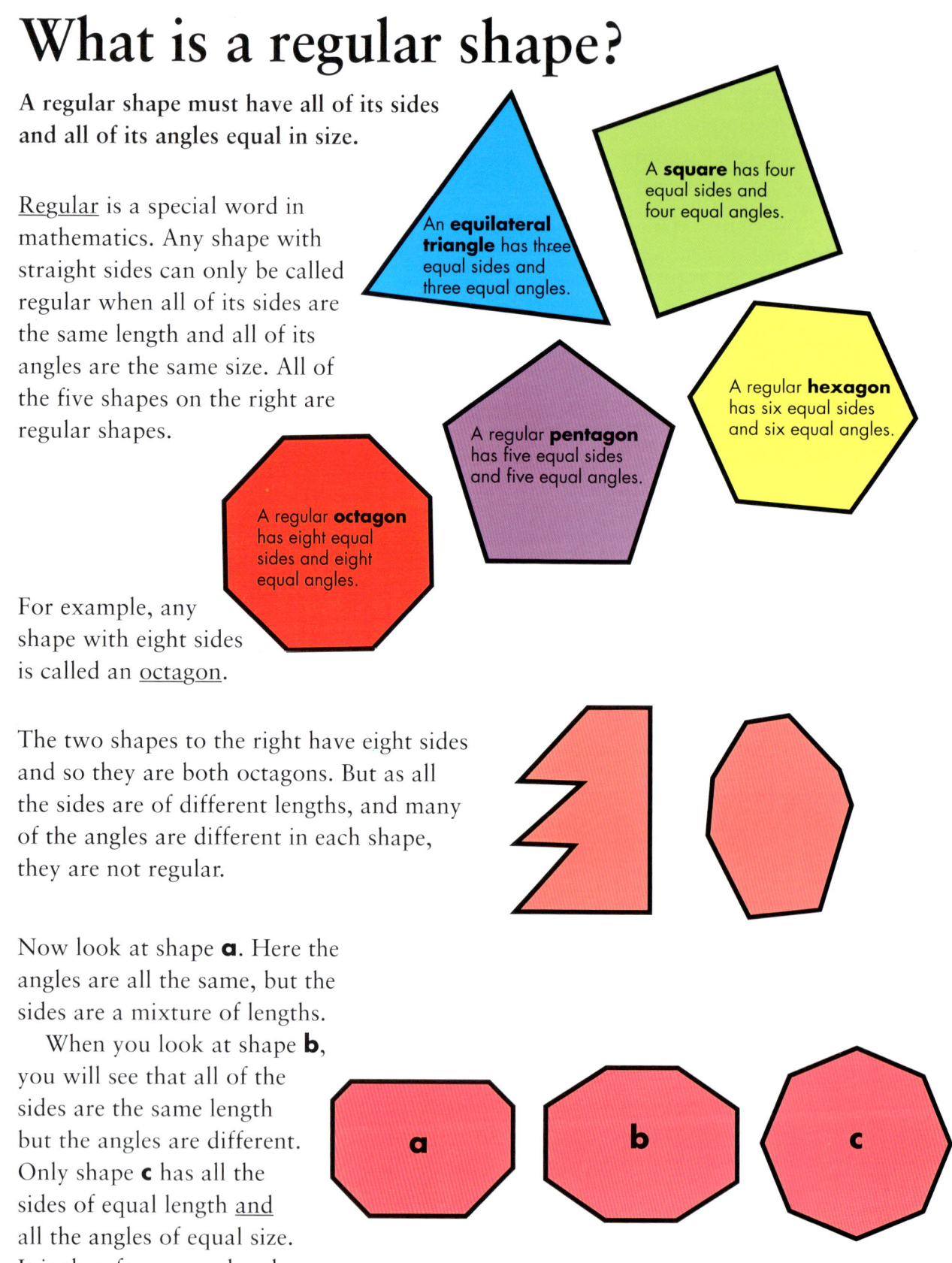

An **equilateral triangle** has three equal sides and three equal angles.

A **square** has four equal sides and four equal angles.

A regular **pentagon** has five equal sides and five equal angles.

A regular **hexagon** has six equal sides and six equal angles.

A regular **octagon** has eight equal sides and eight equal angles.

For example, any shape with eight sides is called an octagon.

The two shapes to the right have eight sides and so they are both octagons. But as all the sides are of different lengths, and many of the angles are different in each shape, they are not regular.

Now look at shape **a**. Here the angles are all the same, but the sides are a mixture of lengths.

When you look at shape **b**, you will see that all of the sides are the same length but the angles are different. Only shape **c** has all the sides of equal length and all the angles of equal size. It is therefore a regular shape.

This stop sign is a regular eight-sided shape called a regular octagon.

This is also an octagon because it has eight sides. But it was actually made from a square with the corners shaved off, so it is not a regular octagon as the sides are unequal.

A quadrilateral is the name for any four-sided shape, but the only regular four-sided shape is a square because all of its sides and angles are equal.

A **quadrilateral** or four-sided shape.

A **square** is the only regular four-sided shape.

Remember… A regular shape must have all of its sides of equal length and all of its angles must be of equal size.

Word check

2D: A two-dimensional shape (2D) has length and breadth but no thickness. Drawings on paper are 2D.

Equilateral triangle: A triangle with sides of equal length and angles of equal size. It is the regular triangle.

Hexagon: A 2D shape with six angles.

Octagon: A 2D shape with eight angles.

Pentagon: A 2D shape with five angles.

Quadrilateral: An entirely straight-sided 2D shape with only four corners.

Regular: A regular 2D shape must have all its sides the same length and all its angles the same size.

Square: A regular rectangle with all four sides the same length and four angles of equal size.

Triangles

Triangles are flat shapes with three angles and three sides.

Look at the green shape on the right. It is called a triangle because it has three (tri) angles. The shape is named after the angles, not the sides.

On the following pages you will find that there are many shapes of triangle, each with its own arrangement of angles.

Why do people use angles and not sides? This is because a triangle can be many sizes, but if the angles remain the same, the triangle will always be the same <u>shape</u>.

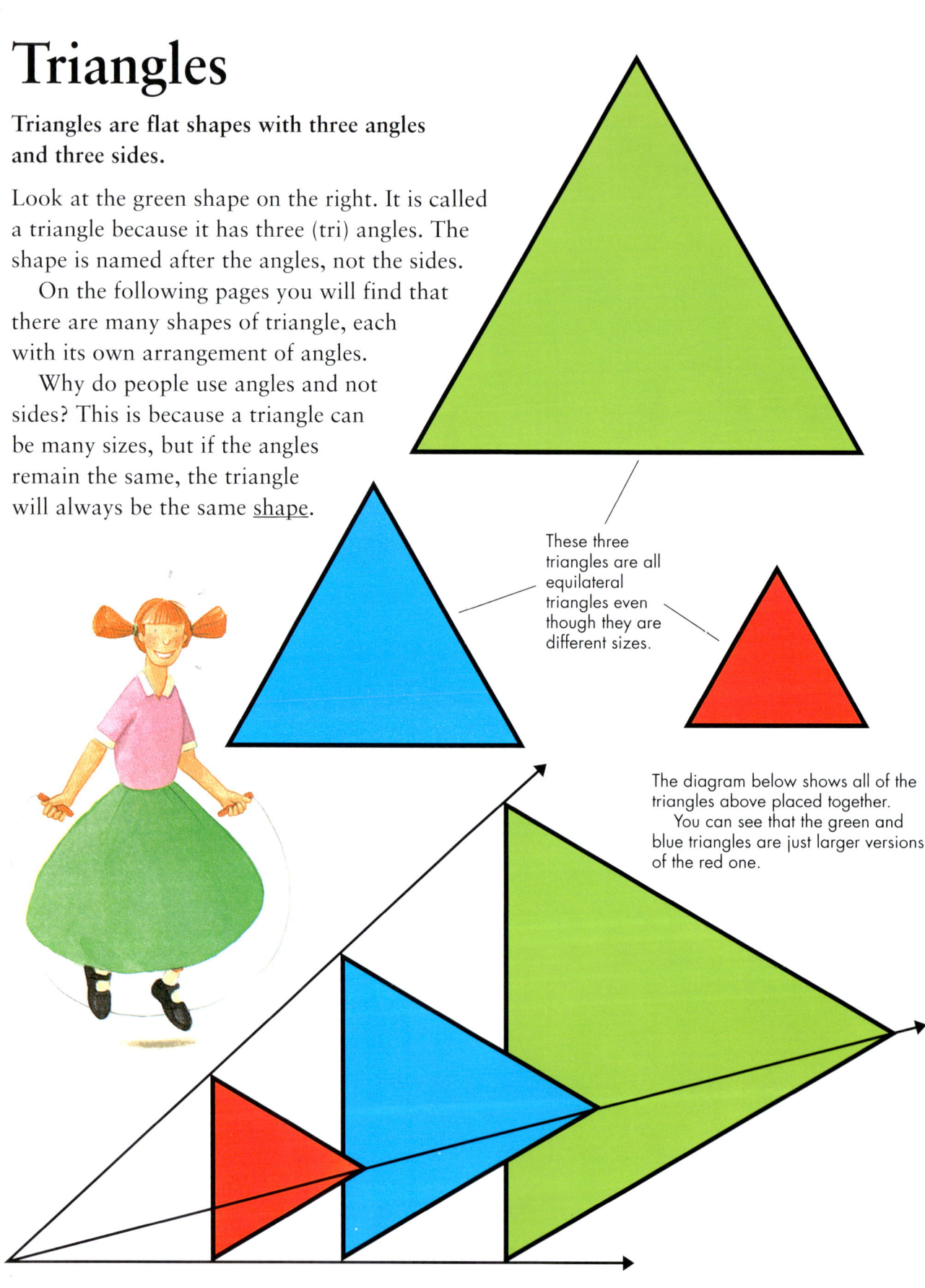

These three triangles are all equilateral triangles even though they are different sizes.

The diagram below shows all of the triangles above placed together.
You can see that the green and blue triangles are just larger versions of the red one.

Properties of any triangle

A triangle is a flat (2D) shape that uses the smallest number of straight lines to enclose a flat surface. A triangle is also the only shape that forms a rigid frame. This important fact is the reason why so many frames for buildings are based on triangles – they will not collapse.

All other straight-sided shapes can be built out of triangles.

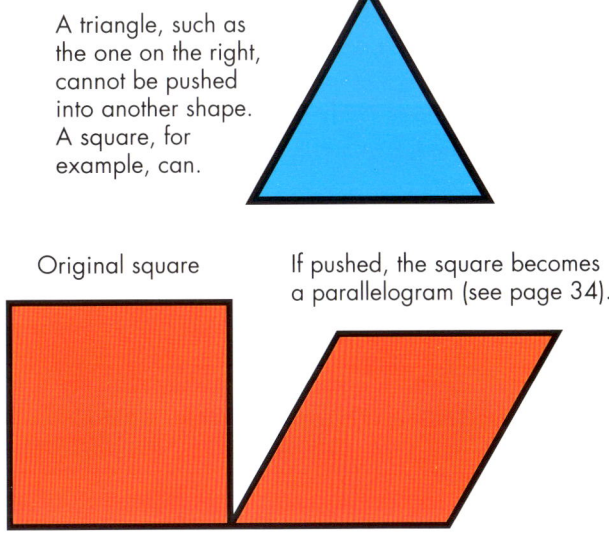

A triangle, such as the one on the right, cannot be pushed into another shape. A square, for example, can.

Original square

If pushed, the square becomes a parallelogram (see page 34).

The three inside angles of a triangle always add up to a half turn.

Book link... To find out more about the inside angles of a triangle, see the book *Size* in the *Maths Matters!* set.

When can you make a triangle?

A triangle can be made of any three lengths, provided that the two shorter lengths (**a** + **b**) add up to more than the longest length (**c**).

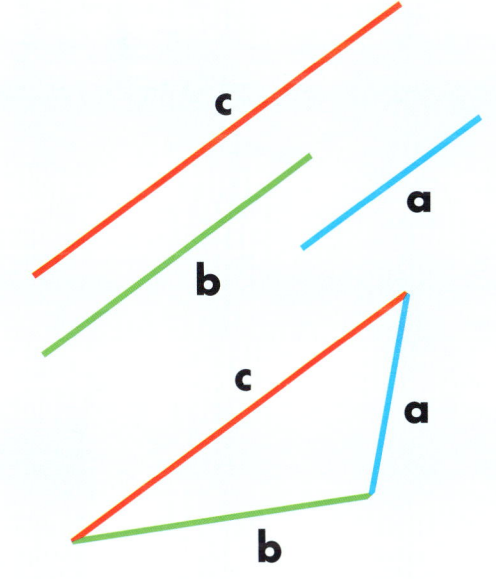

Remember... Only one shape of triangle can be made from any three lengths. The angles do not have to be known. No other shape has this property.

Word check
Triangle: A straight-sided 2D shape with only three corners.

Right-angled triangles

Many triangles have special properties. A right-angled triangle has a right angle (a quarter turn) as one of its angles. In a right-angled triangle the right angle is always the largest angle.

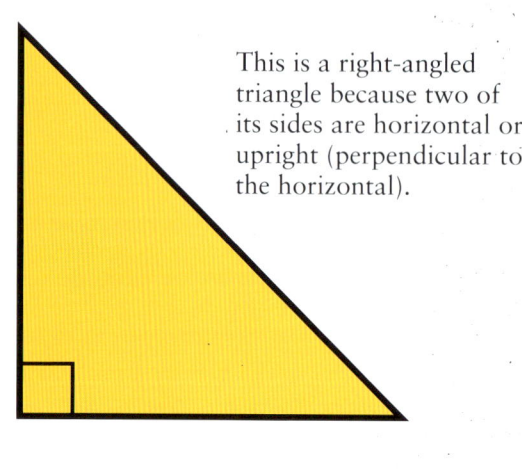

This is a right-angled triangle because two of its sides are horizontal or upright (perpendicular to the horizontal).

Right angles are very common; for example, on the corners of buildings, boxes and books. You can spot a right-angled triangle by placing one of the sides that contains the largest angle level (horizontal). If the triangle is right-angled, the other side will stand exactly upright. Mathematicians say that two lines at right angles are perpendicular.

This is not a right-angled triangle because the second side leans over when the first side is placed horizontally.

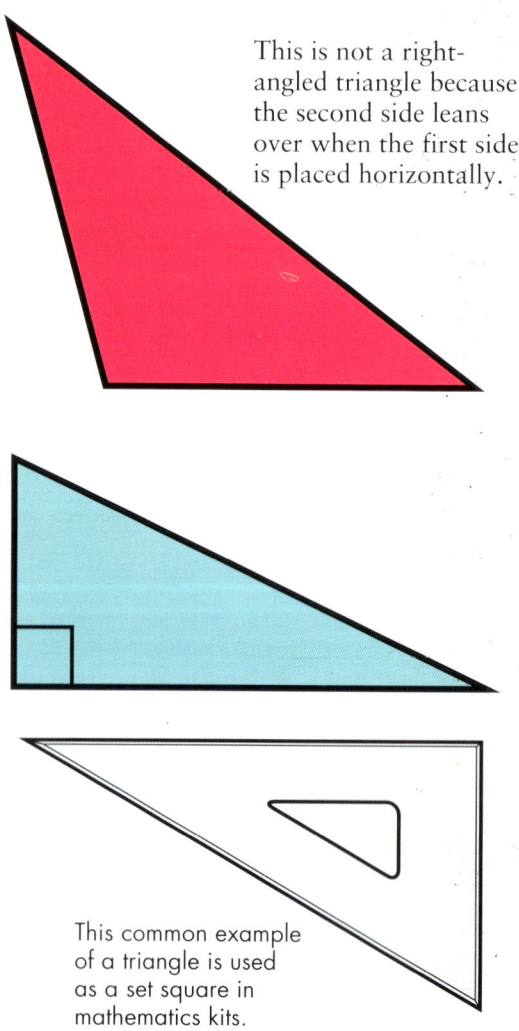

In a right-angled triangle, the other two angles can be the same size as one another or one can be bigger than the other. If the other two angles are the same, each of them is one-eighth of a turn in size.

This common example of a triangle is used as a set square in mathematics kits.

16

The 3-4-5 rule

There is an easy rule to remember that will always help you to draw or mark out a right-angled triangle. It is called the 3-4-5 rule. If you draw a triangle with sides that are 3 units, 4 units and 5 units long (for example 3 cm, 4 cm and 5 cm or 3 inches, 4 inches and 5 inches), they will always form a triangle containing a right angle.

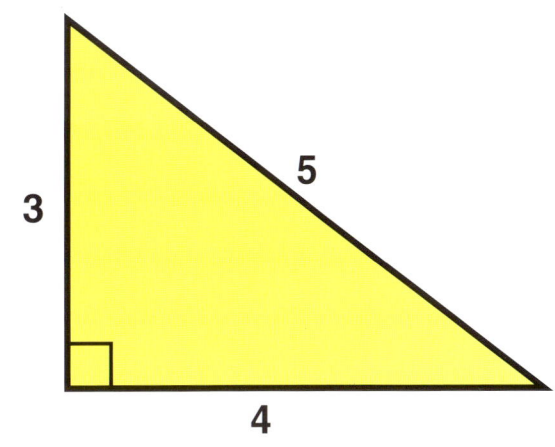

To square up the corner of a model using the 3-4-5 rule

You can use the 3-4-5 rule to make sure that you have made a right angle when you are fastening together two pieces of wood, for example. Measure 3 units (centimetres or inches) from **a** to **b** and 4 units from **a** to **c**. Now get a ruler. Place it across the corner so that it touches **b** and **c**. Check that the ruler measures 5 units between **b** and **c**. If it does, you have a right-angled corner; if it doesn't, gently turn one of the pieces of wood until the ruler shows exactly 5 units.

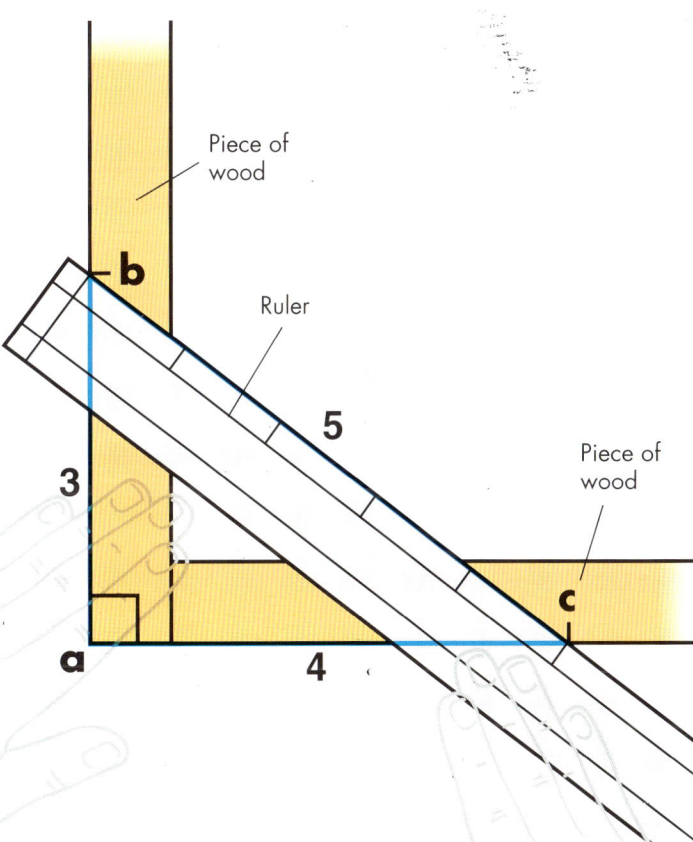

Remember... Right-angled triangles can only be made from special combinations of lengths. The easiest one to remember is 3-4-5.

Word check
Horizontal: Level and flat, like the surface of still water.

Perpendicular: Two lines which meet or cross at right angles are called perpendicular.

Right angle: An angle which is exactly a quarter of a complete turn.

Vertical: Upright, perpendicular to the horizontal.

Triangles with equal angles

Most triangles have three different lengths and three different angles. But some triangles have either three equal angles or two equal angles. Each of these triangles is given a special name and has its own properties.

Two equal angles

A triangle with two equal angles is called an isosceles triangle. It also has two sides of equal length.

This angle is more than 90°, so it is called an obtuse angle.

This is an **isosceles** triangle.

This angle is less than a right angle, so it is called an acute angle.

This is an **isosceles** triangle.

These angles are the same. They are each less than 90°.

Triangles in a circle

You can easily draw an isosceles triangle by using a pair of compasses. Mark out a circle with a radius the same length as the equal sides of the isosceles triangle, then join any two radii.

<u>Any</u> triangle drawn using two radii of a circle will be an isosceles triangle.

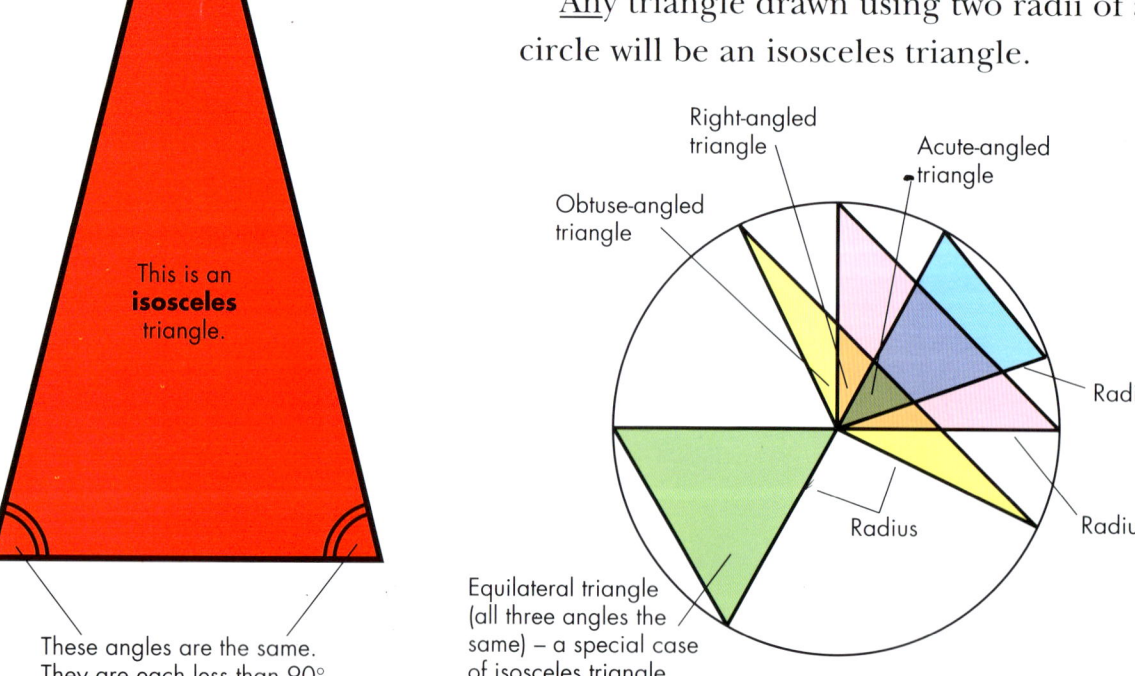

Right-angled triangle

Acute-angled triangle

Obtuse-angled triangle

Radius

Radius

Radius

Equilateral triangle (all three angles the same) – a special case of isosceles triangle.

Three equal angles

A triangle with three equal angles is called an equilateral (regular) triangle. It also has three sides of equal length.

You will see that an equilateral triangle is a special case of an isosceles triangle in which the third side happens to be the same length as the two equal ones. An equilateral triangle is isosceles three ways round. Just turn the triangle around and around to see why.

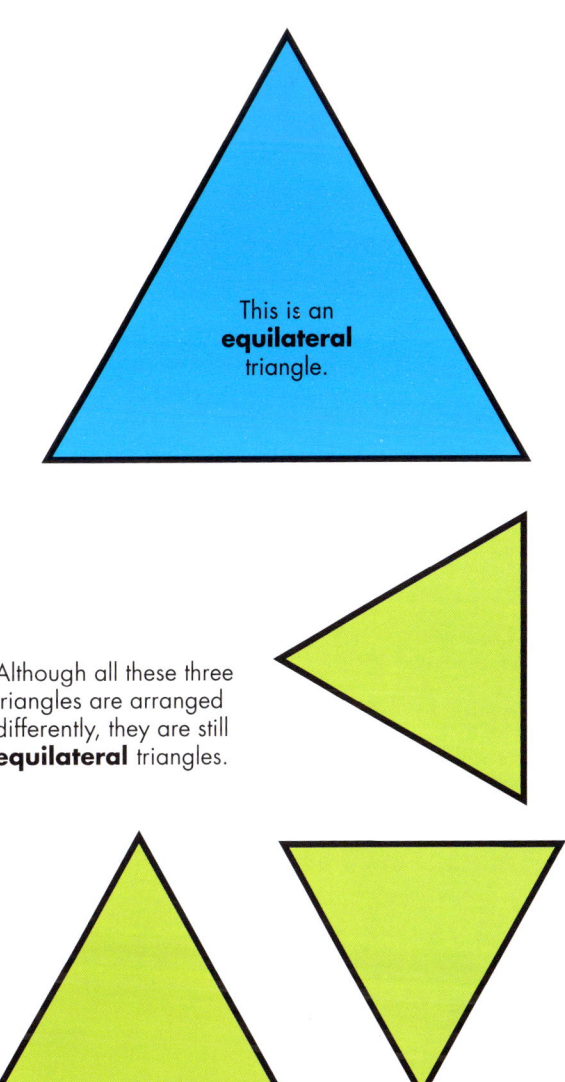

This is an **equilateral** triangle.

Although all these three triangles are arranged differently, they are still **equilateral** triangles.

An equilateral triangle this way up is used as an international warning sign. An equilateral triangle the other way up is an instruction such as 'yield'. Can you spot one near your home?

Remember… Isosceles triangles have two equal angles; equilateral triangles have three equal angles.

Work check

Acute angle: An angle that is smaller than a right angle.

Compasses: An instrument for drawing circles and arcs.

Equilateral triangle: A triangle with sides of equal length and angles of equal size. It is the regular triangle.

Isosceles: A triangle or a trapezium with just two sides the same length is called isosceles.

Obtuse angle: An angle which is larger than a right angle and smaller than a straight angle.

Radius: The distance from the centre of a circle to its boundary. The plural of radius is radii.

How to draw triangles

There are several ways to draw a triangle. Here we show you how to draw one if you know the length of the three sides. You will need a ruler, a protractor and a pair of compasses.

Before you start drawing, always make a rough sketch of the triangle using the information you have. In this way you cannot go far wrong as you draw your triangle.

Drawing a triangle using three sides

Choose one of the lengths to start with. This first side is called the <u>base</u>. It is usually drawn as a horizontal (level) line. Using a ruler and a pencil, draw the base line to the correct length on your paper. In this example the base line is 5 units long.

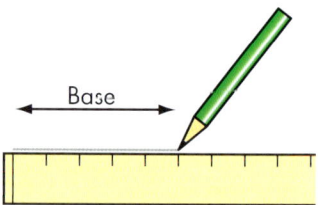

Once it is drawn, it is labelled **A** and **B**.

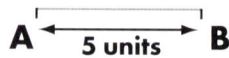

Now, open up a pair of compasses against the ruler until the space between the pointed end and the pencil tip is equal to the length of one of the other sides. In this example it is 4 units.

Place the point of the compasses at the end **A** of the base line and swivel it around, so that the pencil makes a part of a circle, or <u>arc</u>, on the paper.

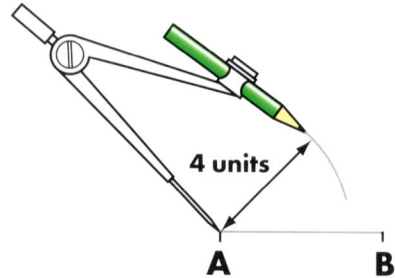

Now set the compasses to the last length using the ruler (**3** units in this example) and place the point at the other end (**B**) of the base line. Draw another arc. This arc will cross the first one at **C**.

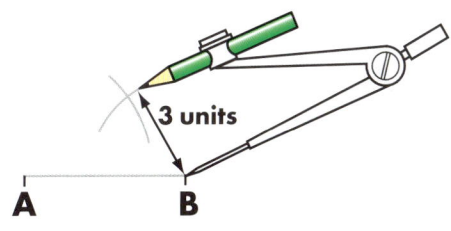

Join the ends of the base line to the point **C** where the arcs cross to complete your triangle. In this case it is a right-angled triangle with sides of **3-4-5**.

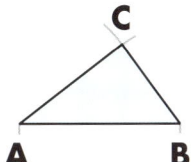

Draw a triangle with three equal sides

An equilateral triangle has all three lengths the same, so set the compasses using the base line and mark two arcs of the same length as the base, one from each end. The angles will all be the same.

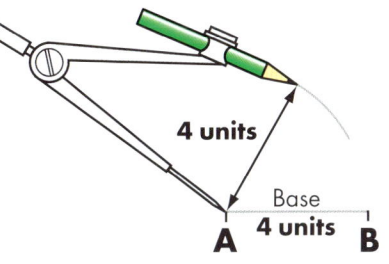

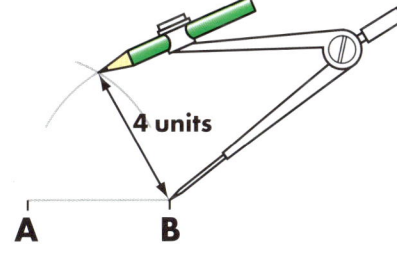

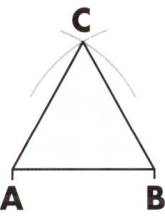

Remember... When trying to draw accurately, keep your pencil sharp and work as carefully as you can. It saves time in the long run.

Word check
Arc: Part of a circle. It is drawn using compasses.
Base: The starting line for drawing a triangle.

Simple symmetry and triangles

Does a shape look the same from more than one direction? Can you fold one part of a shape onto another exactly? If so, the shape has 'symmetry'.

If a shape has symmetry, it can be picked up and turned around, or sometimes turned over, and placed back down again, so that you can't see the difference.

Some shapes have more symmetry than others. However, symmetry is a special feature of some shapes; most shapes have no symmetry at all.

Many animals are symmetrical as you can see by looking at this beetle.

Line of symmetry

Making a symmetrical shape

Take a set square from your mathematics kit and draw around it. Now flip it over and put it against the drawing so that the right angles are together. It makes a new triangle, as you can see below. This means that the shape has flip symmetry.

Flipping a shape like this to make a new symmetrical shape is called a reflection. The new triangle is symmetrical about the vertical side. As a result, the vertical side is called a line of symmetry.

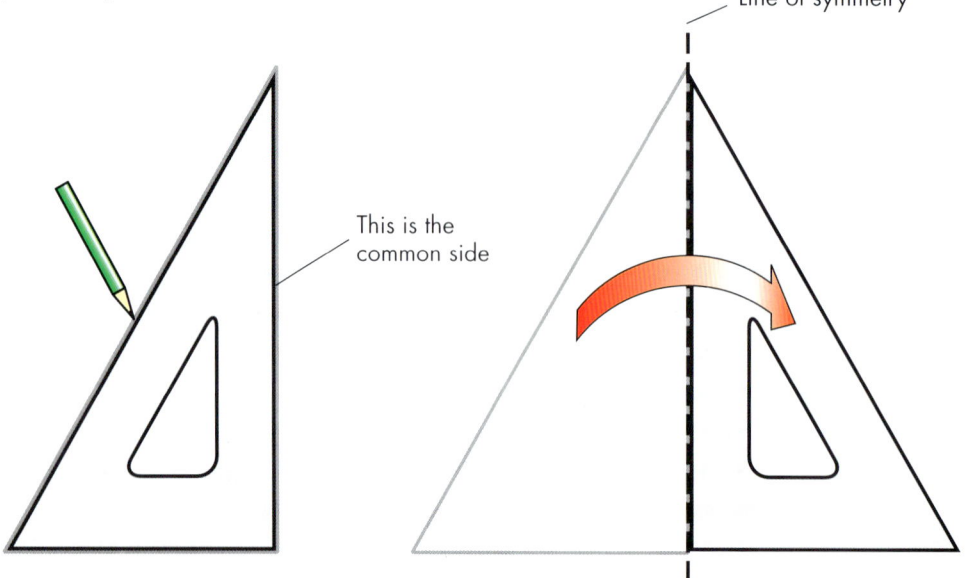

This is the common side

Line of symmetry

This equilateral triangle can be spun around by a third of a turn and it will look exactly the same.

Here you can see how an equilateral triangle can be turned around until it rests on another of its bases. Once turned this way, it looks the same as it did at the starting point. This is an example of turning symmetry.

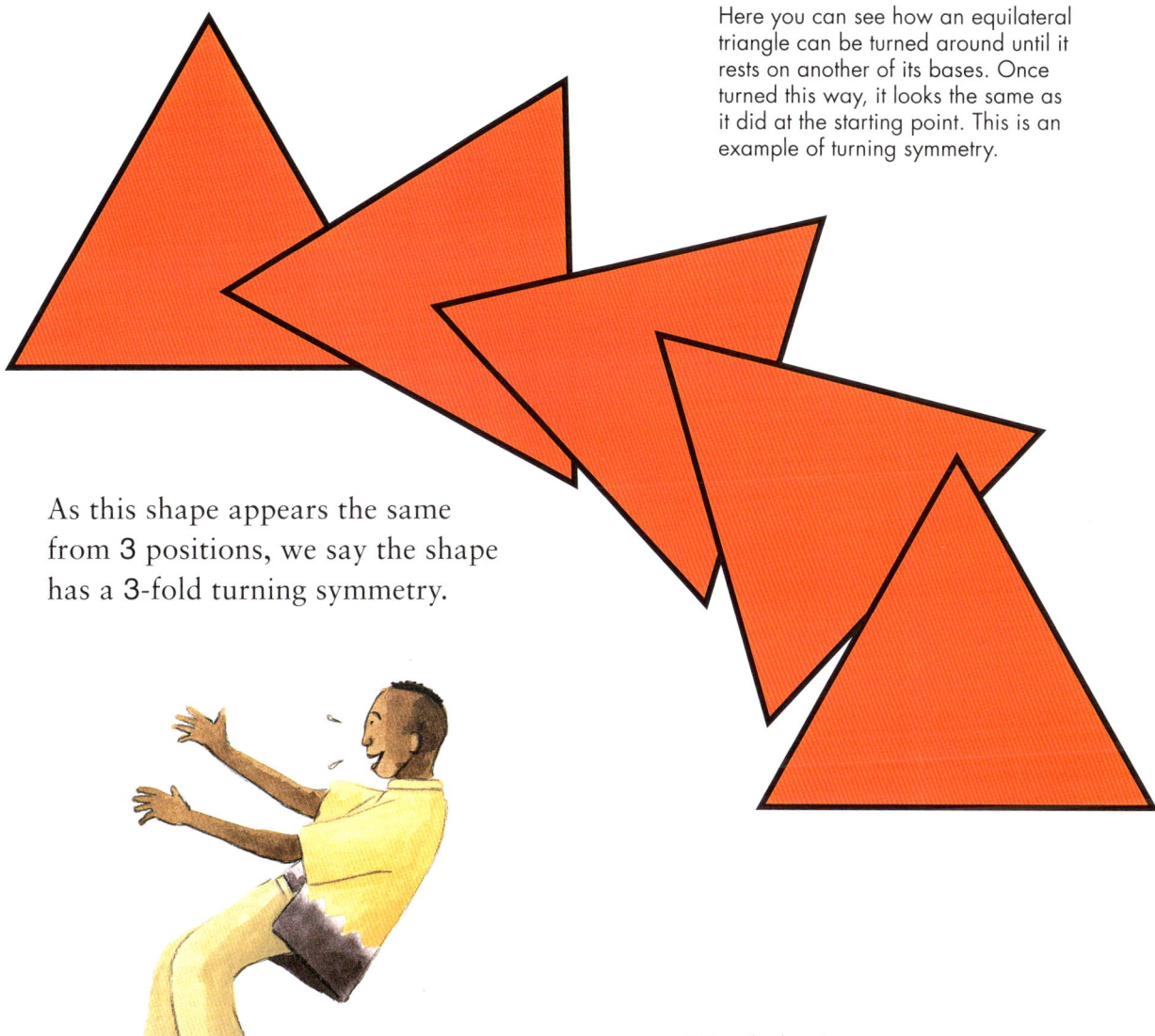

As this shape appears the same from **3** positions, we say the shape has a **3**-fold turning symmetry.

Remember... Symmetry is a word that comes from the Greek, meaning 'same measurements'. All symmetrical shapes therefore have some measurements the same.

Word check
Flip symmetry: A shape which can be flipped over so that it looks just the same.
Reflection: A 'mirror image' of a shape.
Symmetry: The property of a shape that allows it to be turned about a point or flipped over a line and still look just the same.
Turning symmetry: When a pinpoint is pushed through the centre of the shape, it can be turned (less than a complete turn) so that it looks just the same.

Many-fold turning symmetry

Some objects can be placed down in several ways so that you cannot tell they have been moved from their starting position. The more times you can do this, the more 'fold turning symmetry' the object has. You can see this clearly with the examples on this page.

If a shape has turning symmetry, you can push a pin through it and spin it into a new position that looks exactly the same as the starting position.

This star has 4-fold turning symmetry. This is the same symmetry as a square (it also has 4 lines of flip symmetry).

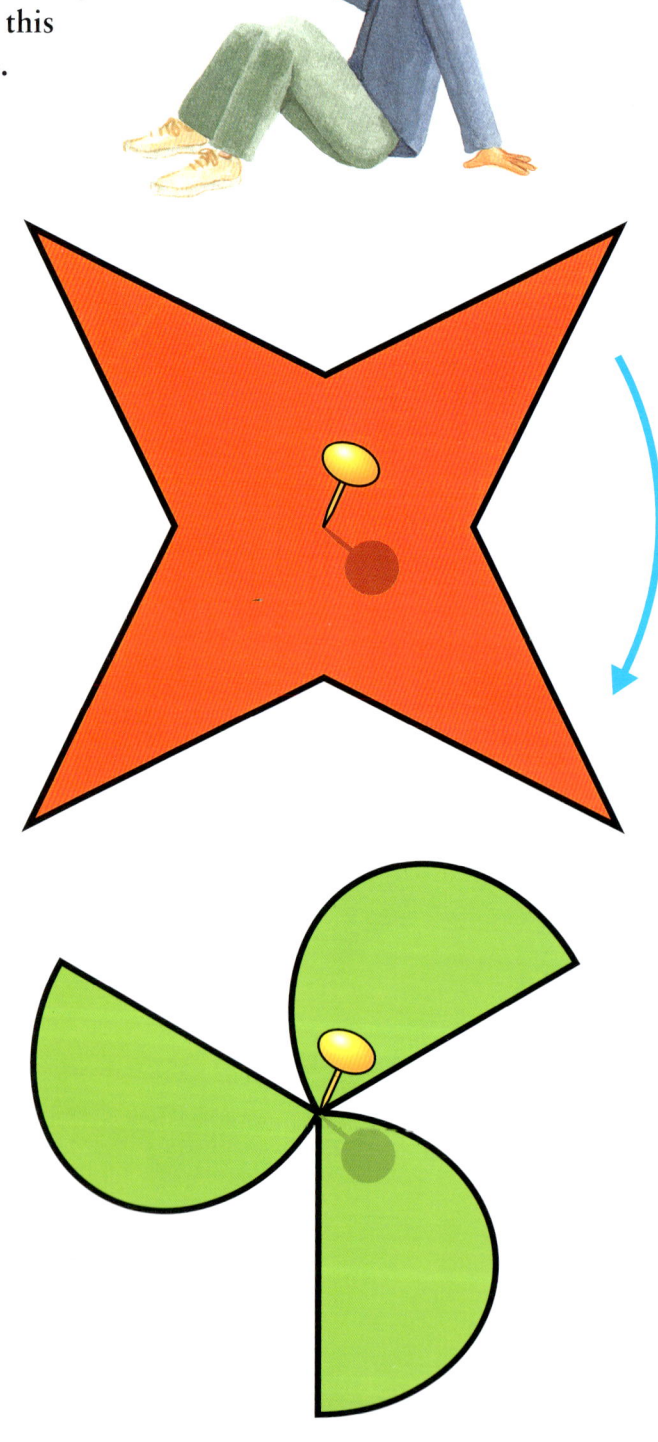

This shape has 3 arms and appears the same from 3 positions. The shape has 3-fold turning symmetry.

A rectangle has **2**-fold turning symmetry (it also has **2** lines of flip symmetry).

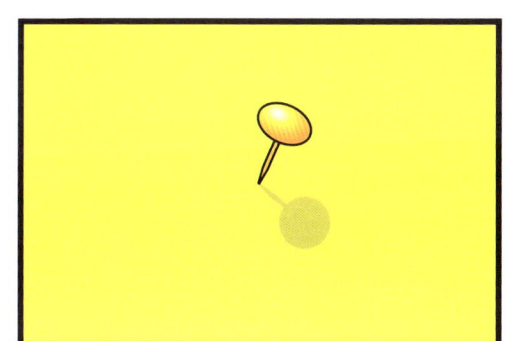

This shape has **4** arms and appears the same from **4** positions. The shape has **4**-fold turning symmetry (it also has **2** lines of flip symmetry).

This star has **20** arms and appears the same from **20** positions. The shape has **20**-fold turning symmetry (it also has **20** lines of flip symmetry).

Remember… Some shapes have only turning symmetry; a few have turning and flip symmetry.

Word check
Many-fold: This describes how many times a shape can be turned about its centre so that it looks just the same before it really comes back to where it started.

Symmetry in letters

Many letters of the alphabet have symmetry. Think about capital letters. Usually, those letters with symmetry are simpler and faster to recognise. Check that this is true by looking at the symmetry of the capital letters on this page. You will also find that, as you look at each letter, you become better at spotting symmetry in other shapes.

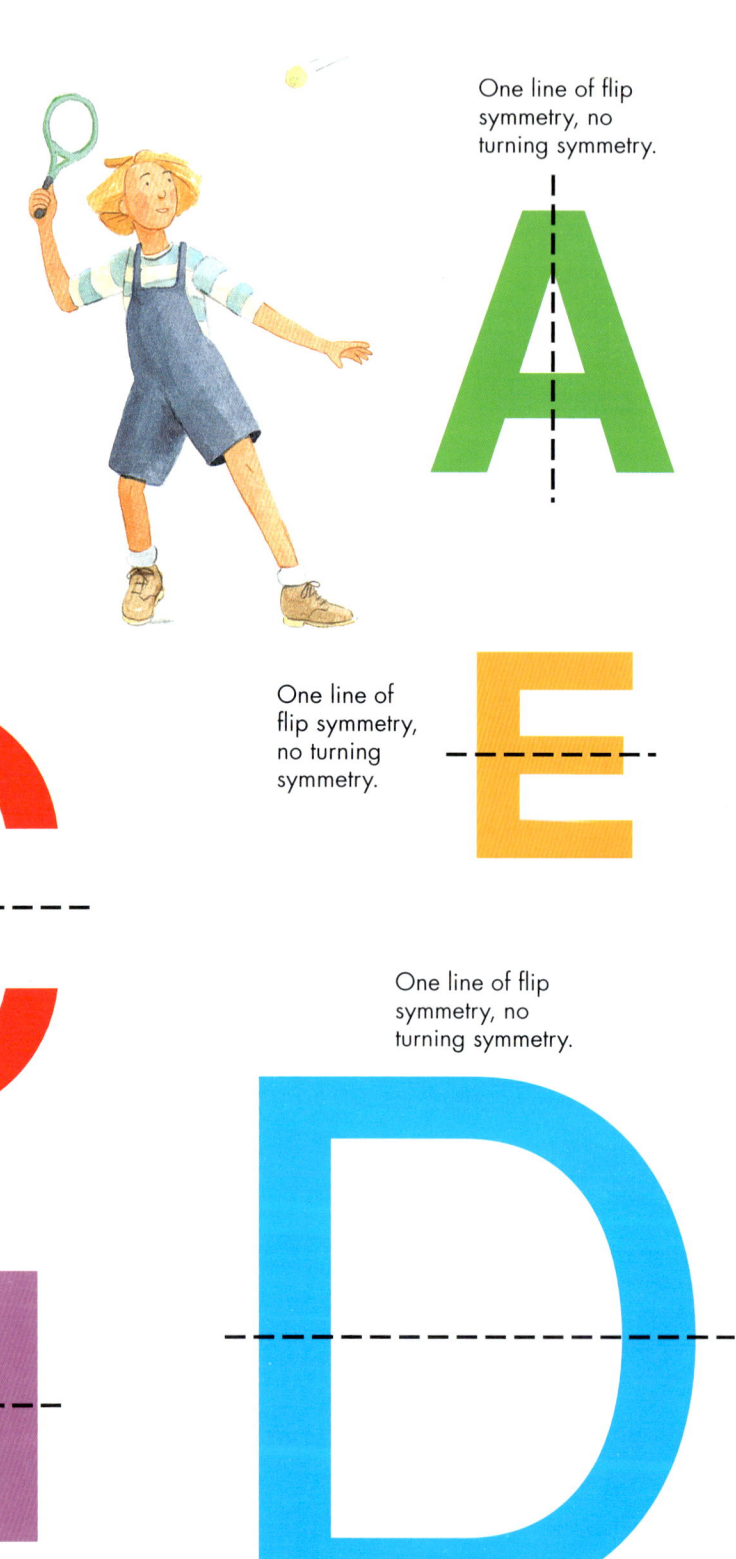

One line of flip symmetry, no turning symmetry. — A

One line of flip symmetry, no turning symmetry. — C

One line of flip symmetry, no turning symmetry. — E

One line of flip symmetry, no turning symmetry. — D

2 lines of flip symmetry and 2-fold turning symmetry. — H

26

2 lines of flip symmetry and 2-fold turning symmetry.

As many lines of symmetry as you like, provided they all go through the centre of the circle. A circle also has as much turning symmetry as you like.

2-fold turning symmetry but no flip symmetry.

2-fold turning symmetry but no flip symmetry.

One line of flip symmetry, no turning symmetry.

You might like to try out U, V, W, X, Y and Z for yourself...

Remember... Some shapes have flip or turning symmetry, while a few have both.

Patterns of interlocking triangles

A pattern of interlocking triangles will completely cover a surface.

If you take a triangle and make many copies of it, you will discover that the triangles can be arranged to cover a surface completely. It does not matter what shape of triangle you start with, the copies will always interlock to cover a surface. Here are three examples to show how it works.

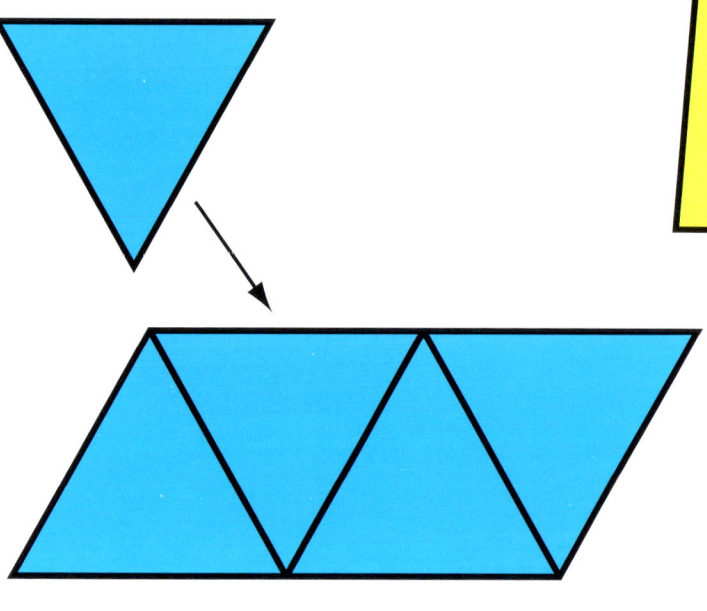

Why it works

The shape covers the surface because:

1. The angles arrange themselves around one central point, so that the sides touch without gaps or overlaps.

2. The sides have matching lengths, so that more central points keep forming for as long as they are needed.

Creating an interlocking pattern of triangles from ruled lines

One way to create a set of interlocking triangles is to draw three sets of straight lines. The steps are shown here.

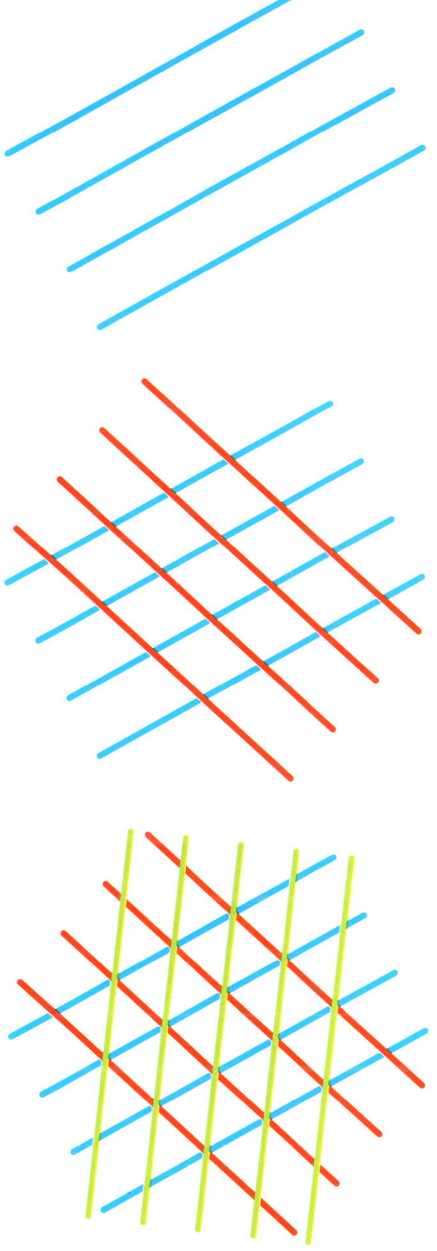

Step 1. Draw any set of equally spaced (parallel) lines.

Step 2. Draw a second set of equally spaced lines at an angle to the first set.

Step 3. Draw a third set of lines through the places where the first two sets of lines cross.

Remember… Only triangles, squares, rectangles (which are used as bricks) and hexagons interlock.

Also… Mathematicians use a special word for shapes that interlock to cover a surface. They say that the shape <u>tessellates</u> a surface.

Word check
Parallel: Parallel lines are lines which will remain the same distance apart for ever.

Tessellate: To make a perfectly interlocking pattern (from the Latin word *tessella*, meaning 'a small stone used to make mosaic decorations').

Quadrilaterals

A quadrilateral is the name given to any flat (2D) shape with four straight sides. The sides do not have to be of equal length.
 There are many special quadrilaterals, and they are known by common names. Examples include squares and rectangles. You can see them here.

Note... For an explanation of the symbols used for the shapes on this page, turn to page 44.

There are some things which are true of all quadrilaterals:

They all have four straight sides.

Lines can be drawn connecting opposite corners. These are called diagonals.

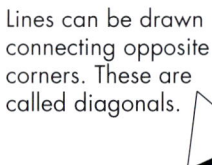

The inside angles (**a**, **b**, **c**, **d** in the diagram below) add up to one complete turn, no matter what shape the quadrilateral is.

a + b + c + d = 1 turn

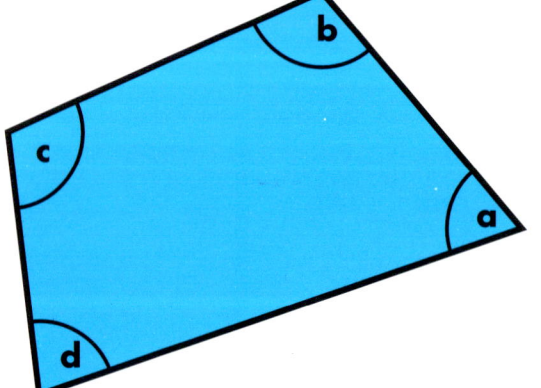

Here are the shapes and properties of all the quadrilaterals you can find. They are shown in more detail on the following pages.

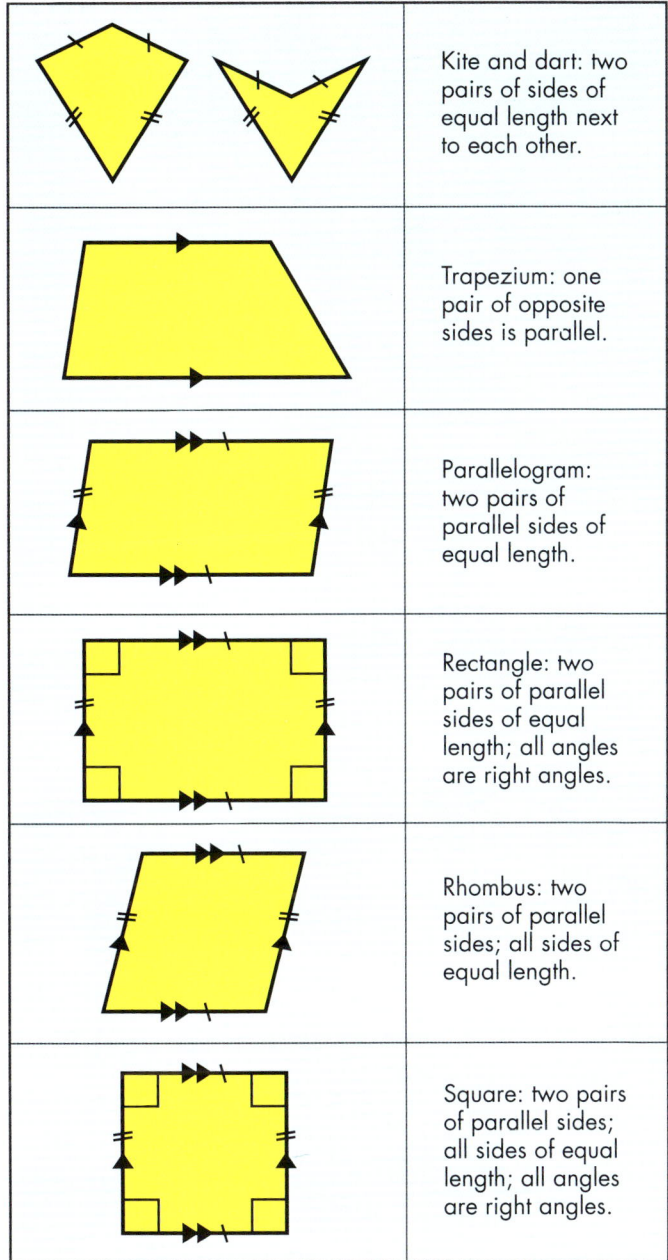

	Kite and dart: two pairs of sides of equal length next to each other.
	Trapezium: one pair of opposite sides is parallel.
	Parallelogram: two pairs of parallel sides of equal length.
	Rectangle: two pairs of parallel sides of equal length; all angles are right angles.
	Rhombus: two pairs of parallel sides; all sides of equal length.
	Square: two pairs of parallel sides; all sides of equal length; all angles are right angles.

Remember… Any four-sided figure is a quadrilateral. The most common quadrilaterals are squares and rectangles.

Word check

Diagonal: A line crossing the inside of a shape from one corner to another.

Inside angle: The smaller angle between the lines at a corner.

Outside angle: The angle at a point measured outside the shape it belongs to.

Quadrilateral: An entirely straight-sided 2D shape with only four corners.

Trapeziums

A trapezium is a four-sided shape where the only rule is that two sides are parallel but of different lengths.

In these diagrams you can see the most common kind of trapezium, where two sides have the same length.

Make a trapezium

To make a trapezium, draw a triangle, and cut a small triangle off the top, as shown on the right. This leaves behind a trapezium.

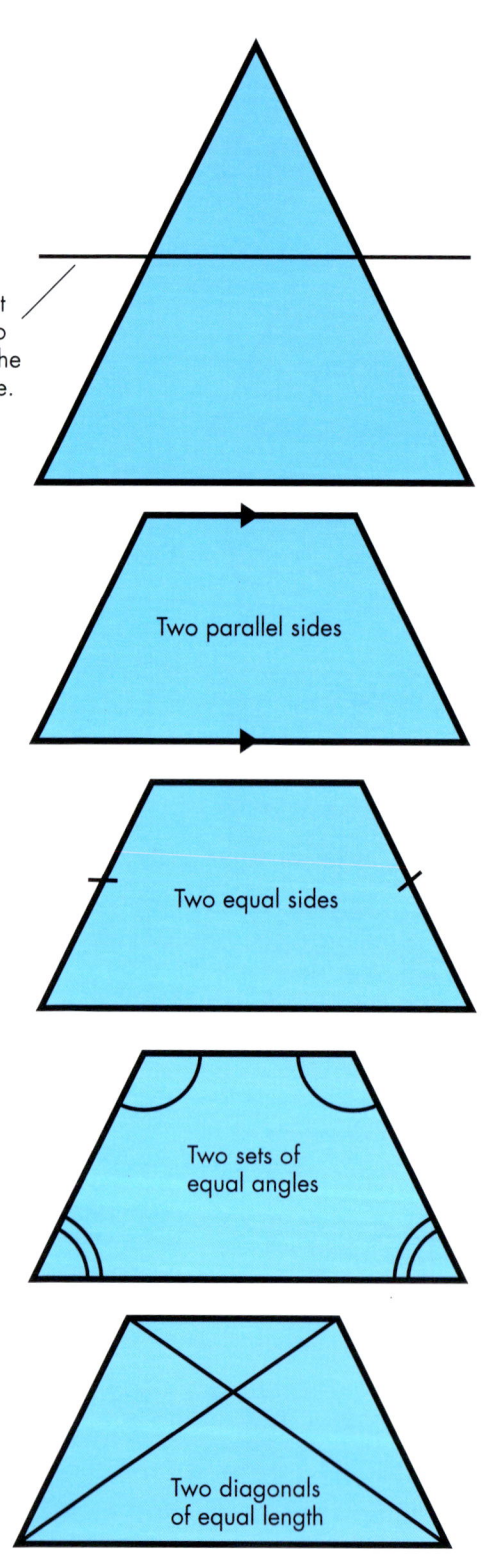

This line must be parallel to the base of the large triangle.

Two parallel sides

Two equal sides

Two sets of equal angles

Two diagonals of equal length

Remember... A trapezium has four sides of differing lengths, but two opposite side must be parallel. This one has been cut from an isosceles triangle, but any triangle can be used.

Word check

Trapezium: A four-sided 2D shape with one pair of parallel sides.

Kites and darts

A kite is a shape with four straight sides and two pairs of touching sides of equal length. A dart is based on the shape of a kite.

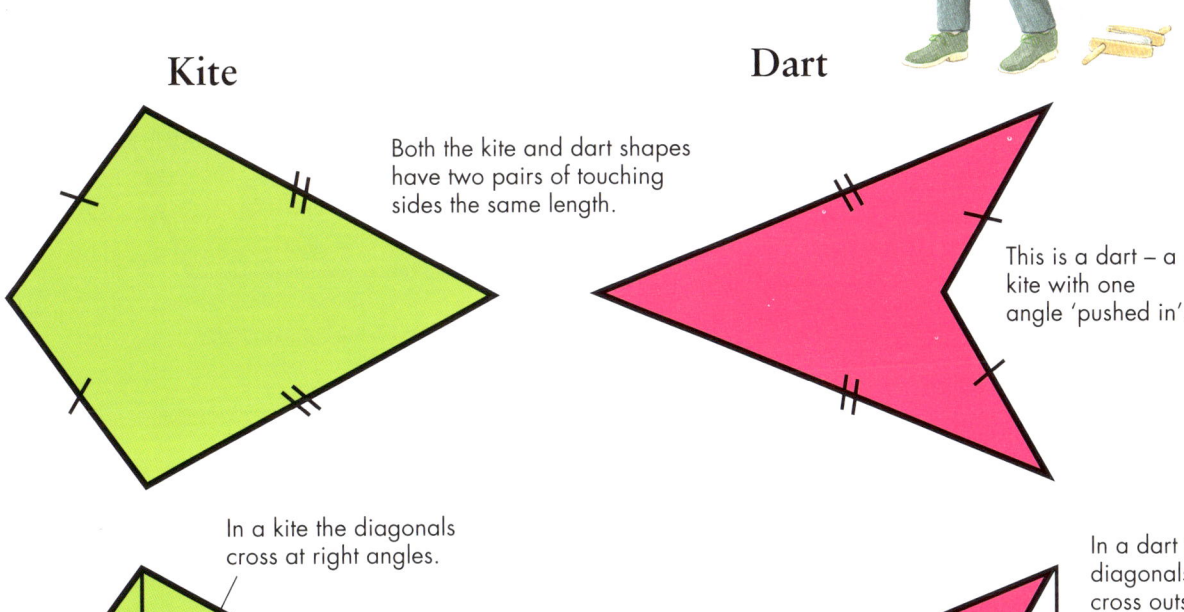

Kite

Dart

Both the kite and dart shapes have two pairs of touching sides the same length.

This is a dart – a kite with one angle 'pushed in'.

In a kite the diagonals cross at right angles.

In a dart the diagonals cross outside the shape.

Remember... A kite and a dart have the same properties, but a kite has one angle pulled out, whereas a dart has the same angle pushed in.

Word check

Dart: A name for a four-sided shape with two pairs of touching sides the same length, which looks like a paper dart or arrowhead.

Kite: A four-sided shape with two pairs of touching sides the same length, which looks like a traditional kite.

Parallelograms

A parallelogram is a four-sided shape with two pairs of opposite sides that are parallel and of the same length.

Parallelogram

A parallelogram (**a**) can be squashed or stretched as shown below.

To keep the sides the same length, the top has to be squashed down (**b**).

To keep the base and top the same distance apart, the sides have to be stretched (**c**).

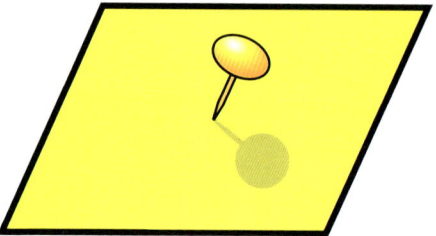

A parallelogram has 2-fold turning symmetry but no flip symmetry.

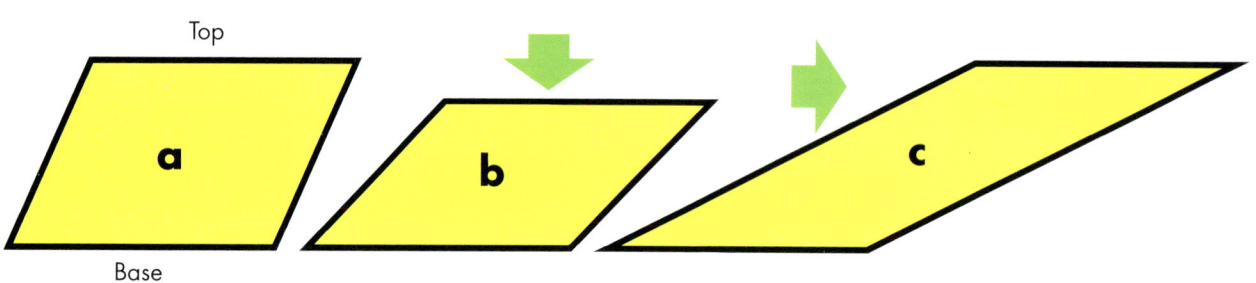

Opposite sides have equal lengths.

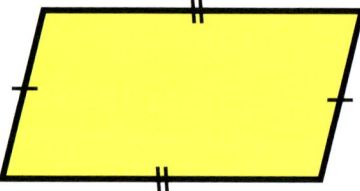

Diagonals cross each other at the half-way point.

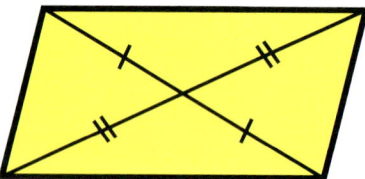

Opposite angles are the same.

Opposite sides are parallel.

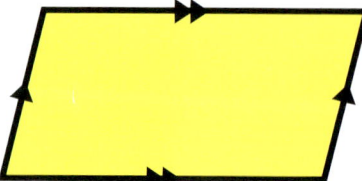

Rhombus

A rhombus is a special kind of parallelogram where the sides are all the same length, but where the sides do not join at right angles.

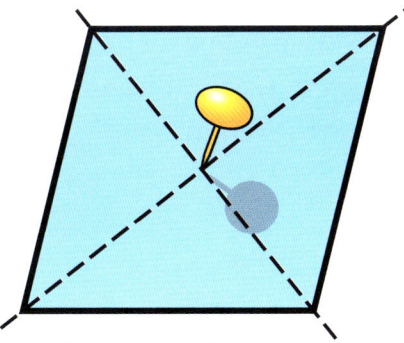

A rhombus has 2-fold turning symmetry. It also has flip symmetry about both the diagonals.

All sides have equal lengths.

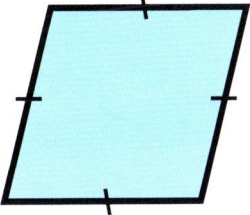

Diagonals cross each other at the half-way point.

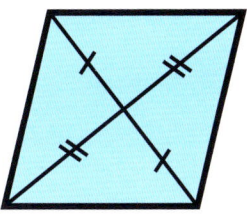

Diagonals cross at right angles and bisect corner angles.

Opposite sides are parallel.

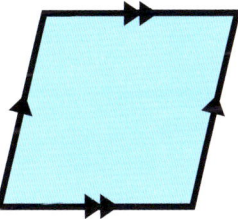

Remember... A parallelogram has two pairs of parallel sides, where each pair can be of different lengths; a rhombus is a special kind of parallelogram where all sides are the same length.

Word check
Bisect: To cut exactly in half.
Parallelogram: A four-sided shape in which opposite sides are parallel.
Rhombus: A four-sided shape with two pairs of parallel sides and all four sides the same length.

Rectangles and squares

A rectangle is a shape with four straight sides and corners that are all right angles.

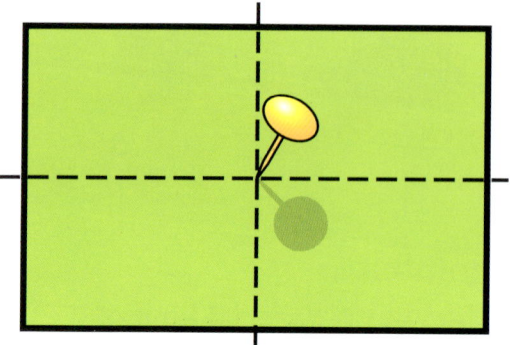

A rectangle has 2-fold turning symmetry, and it has 2 lines of flip symmetry at right angles to the faces.

Rectangle

A rectangle is one of the most common four-sided shapes. It is used to make doors, tables, boxes and so on. All rectangles have right-angled corners. This makes the opposite sides parallel.

Opposite sides have equal lengths.

Diagonals cross each other at the half-way point and are of the same length.

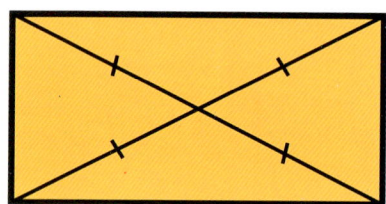

All corner angles are right angles.

Opposite sides are parallel.

The diagram on the right shows that rectangles can be many different shapes. Each of these shapes has the same area, although rectangles can, of course, be many different sizes.

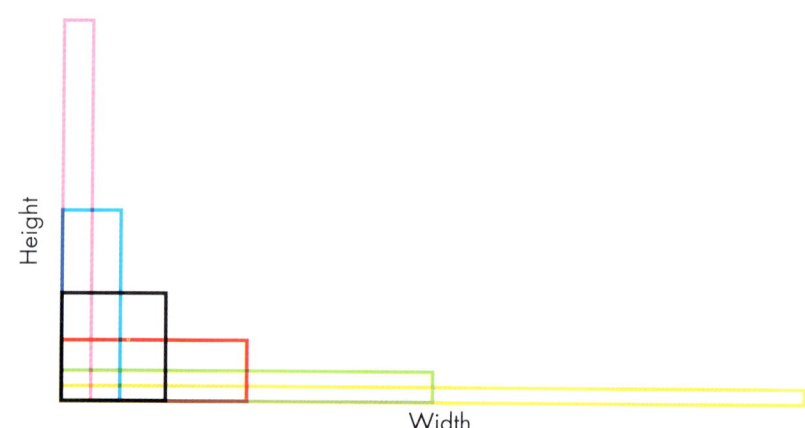

Squares

A square is a rectangle which has all four sides of the same length.

A square is a more symmetrical form of rectangle because all four sides are equal. This means that it has the most symmetry that any four-sided shape could possibly have.

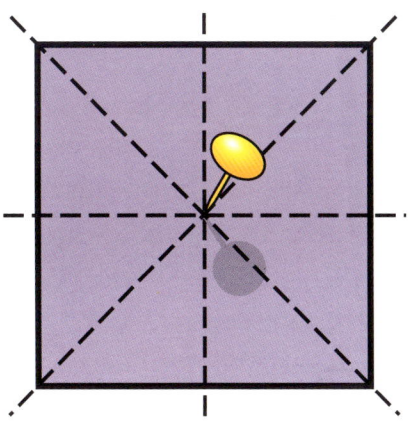

A square has 4-fold turning symmetry, and 4 lines of flip symmetry at right angles to the faces and from each diagonal.

All sides are the same length.

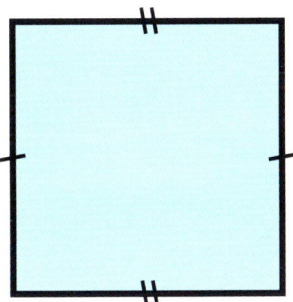

Diagonals cross each other at the half-way point. Diagonals cross at right angles. Diagonals bisect corner angles.

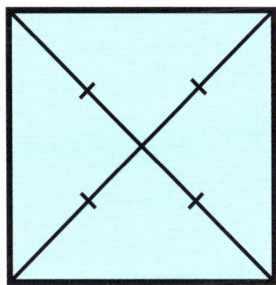

All corner angles are right angles.

Opposite sides are equal lengths and parallel.

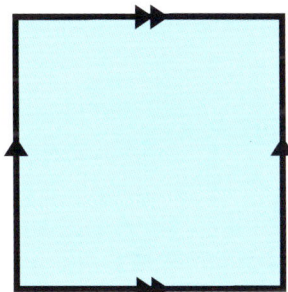

Remember... A square has line symmetry across the edges and the diagonals. It can also be turned or 'rotated' four times about its centre, and so has 4-fold turning symmetry.

Word check

Rectangle: A four-sided shape in which pairs of opposite sides are the same length and all four corners are right angles.

Square: A regular rectangle with all four sides the same length and four angles of equal size.

Ovals and circles

An oval is a shape with an outer edge that is a curve.

A circle is an oval where the curve is all the same. There are no angles to curved shapes.

Of all the flat shapes, the circle is the only one that is perfectly symmetrical. Provided you draw a line across it through its centre, you will always cut it exactly in half. A circle can be turned at any angle and still look the same.

Here are some properties and names of parts of a circle.

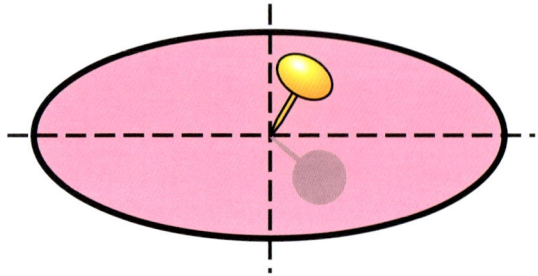

This is an oval. It has two lines of symmetry and it can be turned around on its centre twice, so it has 2-fold turning symmetry and 2-fold flip symmetry.

A circle has many-fold turning and flip symmetry.

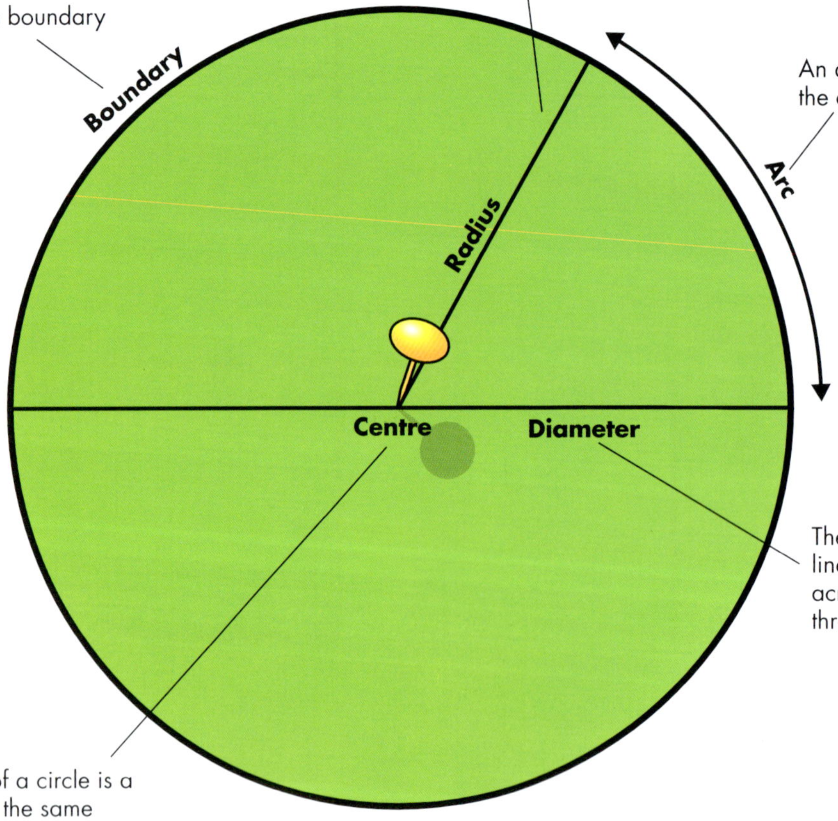

The circumference is the length of the boundary of a circle.

The radius is a line from the centre of a circle to the boundary.

An arc is a part of the circle's boundary.

The diameter is a line drawn right across a circle through its centre.

The centre of a circle is a point that is the same distance in all directions from the boundary. It is half-way along the diameter.

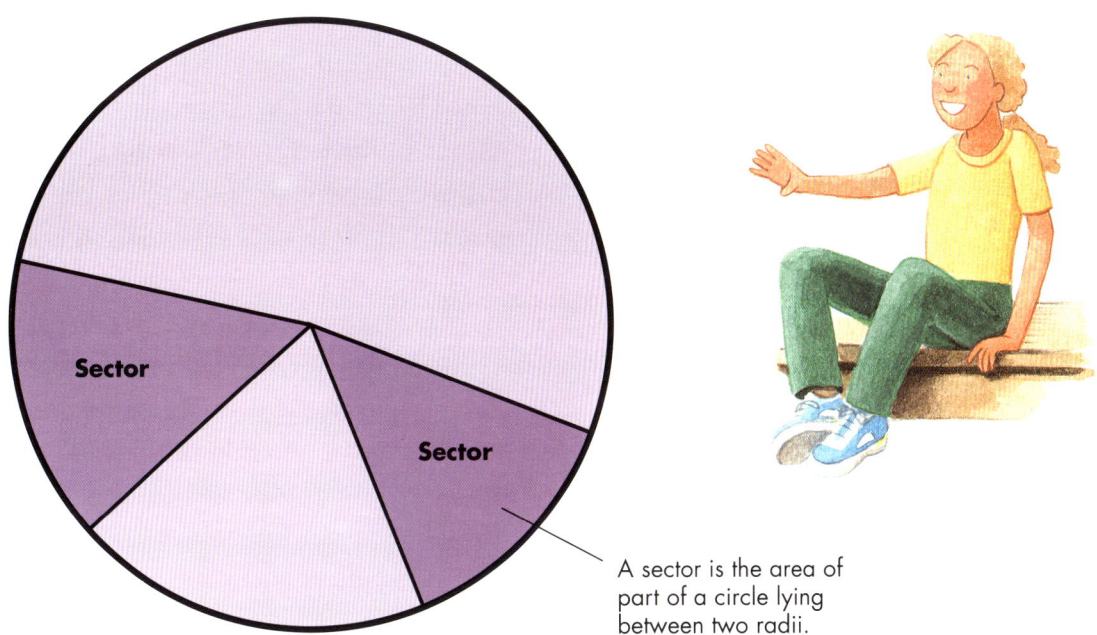

A sector is the area of part of a circle lying between two radii.

Triangles in circles

If you draw triangles inside a circle from the same two places on the circle's boundary, the angles marked with arcs will always be the same size.

If you don't believe this, trace one of the angles and then place it on top of the others in turn.

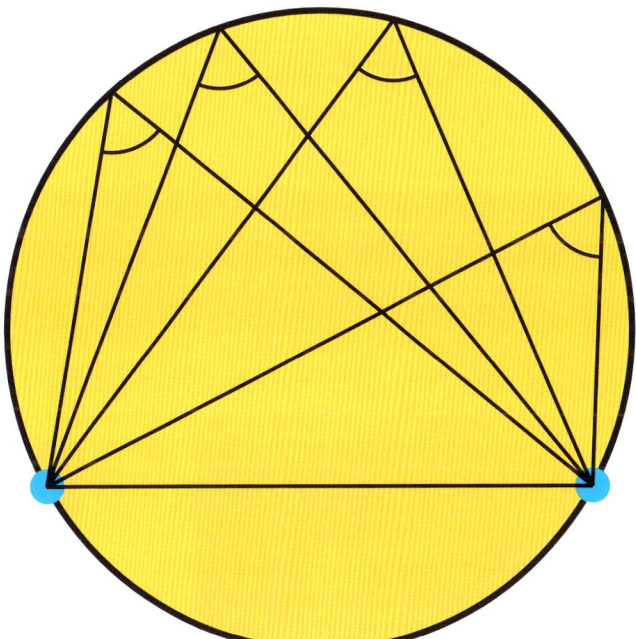

Remember... Circles are the most symmetrical 2D shapes possible.

Word check

Circle: A loop whose boundary is the same distance from the centre all the way round.

Oval: An egg-shaped loop (from the Latin word *ovum*, meaning 'egg'). An oval is usually formed by stretching a circle one way.

Sector: A piece of a circle, like a piece of a pie.

Solid shapes

Solid shapes have depth as well as length and breadth. We say that they are three-dimensional (3D). Some of them are based on simple geometric shapes, as you will see on the following pages.

The starting point is to separate all solid shapes made entirely of flat surfaces – such as cubes – from all those that have curved surfaces – balls (spheres), half-balls (hemispheres), cones, rods and cylinders.

Cubes

A cube is a solid shape with squares for faces. It is therefore a very symmetrical shape. Many natural crystals are cubes.

A cube is also the most useful building block and is widely found in nature.

Making cubes

Many solids can be made by drawing the correct number of flat shapes on paper or card. The design (also called a net) is then used to construct a solid shape.

Tabs are added to alternate edges. Contact adhesive is put on the tabs so that the design can be made up into a solid shape. The ends of the tabs are cut into shallow angles as shown so that they do not get in each other's way. The diagram below is the design you need for a cube.

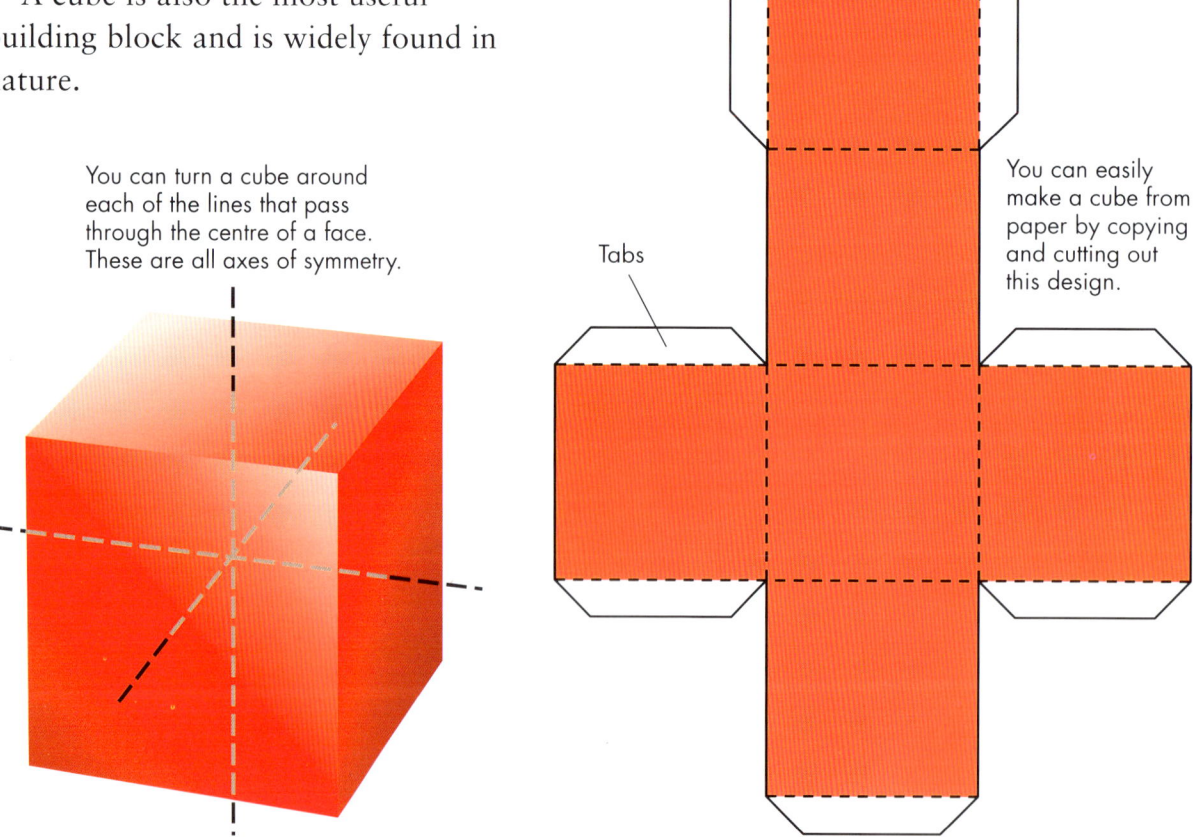

You can turn a cube around each of the lines that pass through the centre of a face. These are all axes of symmetry.

Tabs

You can easily make a cube from paper by copying and cutting out this design.

Pyramids

A pyramid is a solid shape with its sides made up of triangles.

In the more common pyramids the base is a regular flat shape. The pyramids at Giza, Egypt, are square-based pyramids.

If the height of the base to the apex is carefully adjusted, the sloping triangular sides can be made into equilateral triangles.

If all the faces of a triangular-based pyramid are regular (equilateral), then the solid formed is called a regular tetrahedron.

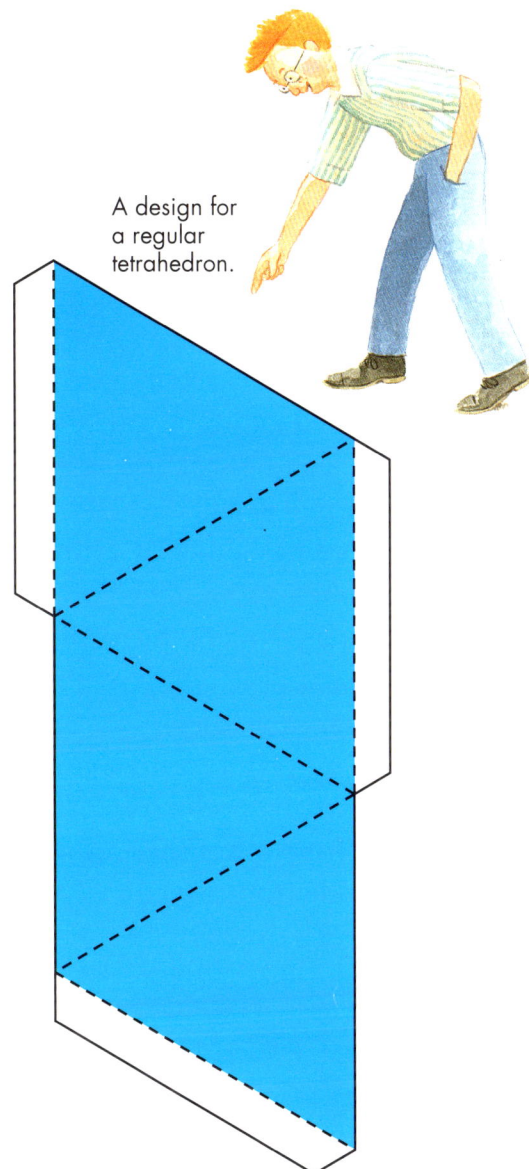

A design for a regular tetrahedron.

When the apex is right above the centre of the base, the triangles are isosceles.

Apex
Edge
Face
Vertex

Remember... Solid shapes have boundaries that are called 'faces' and 'edges', compared with flat shapes that have boundaries called 'lines'.

Word check

3D: A three-dimensional shape (3D) has length and breadth and thickness (depth). It can be solid, just a surface, or even an open framework, like a pylon.

Apex: The highest point of a solid shape at which three or more surfaces meet.

Cube: A 3D shape in which all six faces are squares.

Face: A 2D flat (not curved) surface of a solid. A cube has six faces, for example.

Polyhedron: A general word for an entirely straight-edged 3D shape.

Tetrahedron: A 3D shape with four faces, all triangles (from the Greek *tetra*, meaning 'four').

Vertex: A point at which two lines cross or meet. Also a point at which three or more edges meet.

Cylinders and cones

A cone is a circular pyramid, and a cylinder is a hollowed out rod.

Rods and cylinders both have a circle for their base. When a cylinder is a solid, with its thickness measuring much less that its diameter, (for example, a coin), it is often called a disc. A solid cylinder which has a length much greater than its diameter is often called a rod.

When a rod has a hollow cylinder running through its middle, it might be called a pipe or a tube if the wall is thin. A disc with a hollow centre might be called a ring or a washer.

A cone is a pyramid with a circle for its base. Cones, like cylinders, can be made easily from a flat sheet of paper. A cone is made from a sector of a circle.

By drawing a smaller circle with the same centre inside the base circle, it is easy to make a cone with part of its top removed. Buckets, funnels and some lampshades are made in this way from flat sheets of material.

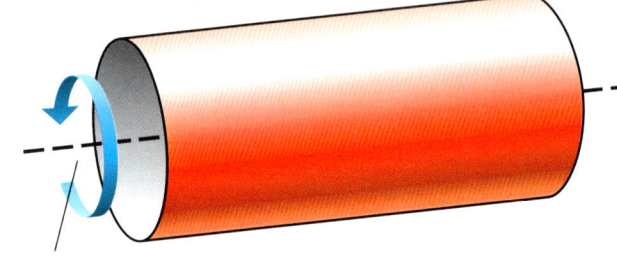

A cylinder is the easiest shape to make from a piece of paper. To make a cylinder, simply roll up a sheet of paper.

Turning symmetry about this axis.

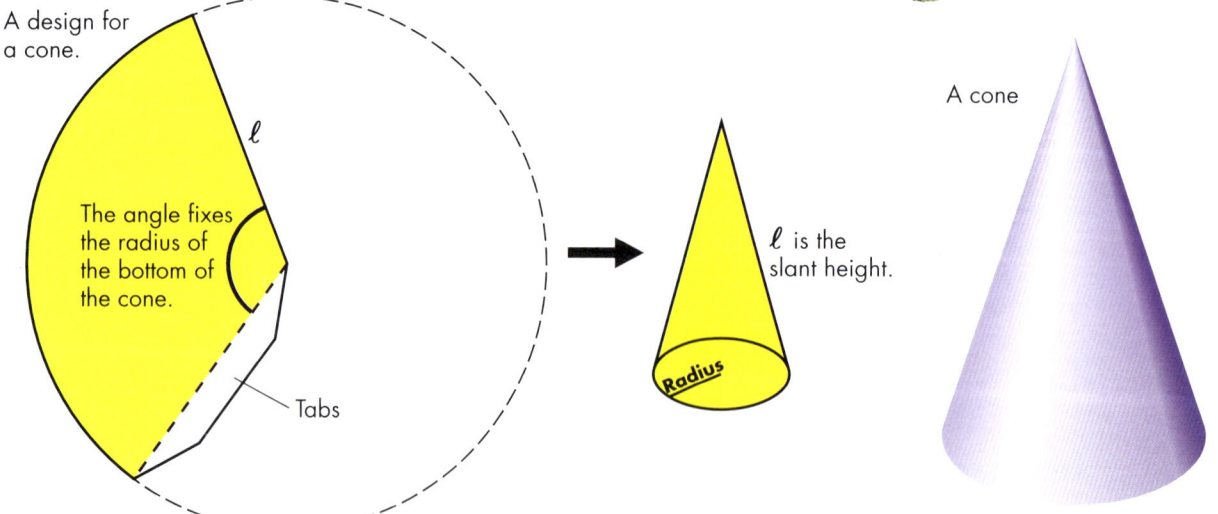

A design for a cone.

The angle fixes the radius of the bottom of the cone.

ℓ

Tabs

ℓ is the slant height.

Radius

A cone

Spheres

Just as a circle is a perfectly symmetrical flat shape, so a sphere is a perfectly symmetrical solid shape.

A sphere is a solid in which every point on the surface is the same distance from the centre.

Spheres cannot be made from flat sheets of paper.

A sphere can have as many symmetries as you wish and is the same shape whichever way you look at it. A given amount of material packs into the smallest possible space when it is made into a sphere.

A ball is a sphere and so it too is the same shape whichever way you hold it. This property allows you to play games with it or use it as ball bearings. Spheres are very useful in the everyday world.

A football is a sphere made with a pattern on the surface. The football on the right is made up of curved patterns of hexagons and pentagons. It has a very large number of symmetries. On this diagram we have shown only two axes. You can see that there will be many more axes such as these. Even so, the use of pentagons and hexagons reduces the symmetry of the sphere.

A sphere

There is 6-fold turning symmetry about the axis of this hexagon.

There is 5-fold turning symmetry about the axis of this pentagon.

Word check

Cone: A pyramid with a circle for a base. It may be solid or just a surface.

Cylinder: A 3D shape that can be made by, for example, rolling up a piece of paper. It may be solid – in which case it is a rod – or may be hollow.

Disc: A solid cylinder whose thickness is much less than its diameter.

Rod: A solid cylinder which has a length much greater than its diameter.

Sector: A piece of a circle, like a piece of a pie.

Sphere: A 3D shape made by spinning a circle around a diameter. It may be solid or just a surface.

Remember… Cones, cylinders and spheres are all formed from circles.

What symbols mean

Some common geometry symbols together with an example of how they are used:

Right angle (90°).

Curves in angles show that the angle is larger than, or less than, a right angle.

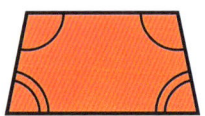
Angles with the same number of curves are the same size.

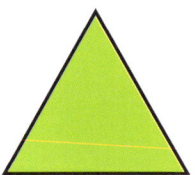
Outer line: The boundary of a shape.

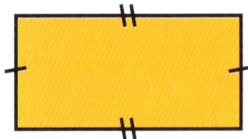
Ticks: Lines (sides or diagonals) with the same number of ticks are the same length.

Arrowheads: Sides with the same number of arrowheads are parallel.

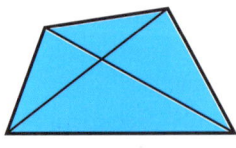
Diagonal lines: A line crossing the inside of a shape from one corner to another.

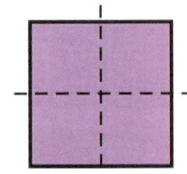
Dashed lines show lines of flip symmetry.

Some common maths symbols:

+ Between two numbers this symbol means 'plus' and is the symbol for adding. In front of one number it means that the number is a plus number. In Latin *plus* means 'more'.

− Between two numbers this symbol means 'subtract' or 'minus'. In front of one number it means the number is a minus number. In Latin *minus* means 'less'.

× The symbol for multiplying. We say it 'multiplied by' or 'times'.

—, / and **÷** Three symbols for dividing. We say it 'divided by'. A pair of numbers above and below a / or − make a fraction, so ⅖ or $\frac{2}{5}$ is the fraction two-fifths.

= The symbol for equals. We say it 'equals' or 'makes'. It comes from a Latin word meaning 'level' because weighing scales are level when the amounts on each side are equal.

. This is a decimal point. It is a dot written after the units when a number contains parts of a unit as well as whole numbers.

( ) The symbols for brackets. You do everything inside the brackets first. Brackets always occur in pairs.

% : The symbol for per cent.

Glossary

This glossary contains the Word check items from earlier in the book along with many other terms commonly used in mathematics.

Acute angle: An angle that is smaller than a right angle.

Apex: The highest point of a solid shape at which three or more surfaces meet.

Arc: Part of a circle. It is drawn using compasses.

Area: The size of the shape within a boundary. It is measured in square units by counting how many unit squares can be fitted into it.

Arms: The arms of an angle are the two lines which meet at a vertex.

Base: The starting line for drawing a triangle.

Bisect: To cut exactly in half.

Boundary: The line or curve separating the inside of the shape you are interested in from everything outside it.

Capacity: The maximum volume that a container can hold. It is measured in special units such as pints or litres.

Chart: A diagram used to show data from tables. There are many kinds of charts, including bar charts and pie charts. *See* Graph.

Circle: A loop whose boundary is the same distance from the centre all the way round.

Circumference: The perimeter of a circle. In Latin *circum* means 'around' and '-ference' comes from a word meaning 'carrying'.

Column: Things placed one below the other. In a table, the entries which are in a line that goes up and down the page.

Compasses: An instrument for drawing circles and arcs. It has two arms jointed at the top. One arm has a pin for the centre of the circle. The other arm has a pencil or pen to draw the circle.

Cone: A pyramid with a circle for a base. It may be solid or just a surface.

Convert: To change one measurement system into another.

Corner: A place where two lines meet. A square has four corners, each made where neighbouring sides meet. The word corner is also often used for triangles. *See* Vertex.

Cube: A 3D shape in which all six faces are squares.

Cubic unit: The same volume as is contained in a unit cube. It can be any shape.

Cuboid: A 3D shape with six faces that are all rectangles; some but not all may be squares.

Cylinder: A 3D shape that can be made by, for example, rolling up a piece of paper. It may be solid – in which case it is a rod – or may be hollow.

Dart: A name for a four-sided shape with two pairs of touching sides the same length, which looks like a paper dart or arrowhead.

Data: Information from which you start to solve a problem. You might have collected it yourself or have been given it. The word comes from Latin meaning 'things given'.

Decimal number: A number that contains parts of units as well as whole units. The decimal point is used to separate the units from the parts of a unit.

Decimal place: The digits used for parts of a unit, such as tenths and hundredths. For example, if a number is given to '2 decimal places', it means that there are digits in the tenths and hundredths columns.

Decimal point: A dot written after the units when a number contains parts of a unit as well as whole numbers.

Degree: A small part of a complete turn. There are 360 degrees in a complete turn.

Diagonal: A line crossing the inside of a shape from one corner to another.

Diameter: The size of a circle measured straight across through its centre. In Greek, *dia* means 'through' and *metria* means 'measurement'.

Disc: A solid cylinder whose thickness is much less than its diameter.

Edge: The line formed where two faces of an object meet.

Equation: A number sentence using the = symbol, telling us that two different ways of writing a number are the same. For example, 2 + 2 = 4 and 9 − 5 = 4.

Equilateral triangle: A triangle with sides of equal length and angles of equal size. It is the regular triangle.

Even number: A multiple of 2.

Exterior angle: The angle that is 180° minus the interior angle. The interior and exterior angle at a point thus make a straight angle. *See* Outside angle and Interior angle.

External angle: The larger angle at a corner. For example, the exterior angle at a corner of a rectangle is 270°; the interior angle is 90°. *See* Outside angle and Interior angle.

Face: A 2D flat (not curved) surface of a solid.

Flip symmetry: A shape which can be flipped over so that it looks just the same.

Formula: A rule for calculating something. It is often an equation containing a letter or several letters.

Grid: A pattern of lines that cross at right angles that is used to make it easier to set out your work.

Hexagon: A 2D shape with six angles.

Horizontal: Level and flat, like the surface of still water.

Inside angle: The smaller angle between the lines at a corner. For example, the inside angle at a corner of a rectangle is 90°, the outside angle is 270°. *See* Interior angle, Exterior angle, External angle and Outside angle.

Intercept: The point where a line graph crosses the y-axis. It is the amount the line is lifted above a parallel line through the origin.

Internal (interior) angle: The smaller angle made where two lines meet. *See* Exterior angle, External angle and Inside angle.

Isosceles: A triangle or a trapezium with just two sides the same length is called isosceles.

Kite: A four-sided shape with two pairs of touching sides the same length, which looks like a traditional kite.

Line: A continuous mark made on a surface. It may be straight or curved, and it can go on for ever in both directions.

Many-fold: This describes how many times a shape can be turned about its centre so that it looks just the same before it really comes back to where it started.

Obtuse angle: An angle which is larger than a right angle and smaller than a straight angle.

Octagon: A 2D shape with eight angles.

Odd number: A number that cannot be divided by 2.

One-digit number: A number between 1 and 9.

Origin: The point where the axes of a graph cross.

Outside angle: The angle at a point measured outside the shape it belongs to. *See* Exterior angle, External angle, Inside angle, Interior angle.

Oval: An egg-shaped loop (from the Latin word *ovum*, meaning 'egg'). An oval is usually formed by stretching a circle one way.

Parallel: Parallel lines are lines which will remain the same distance apart for ever.

Parallelogram: A four-sided shape in which opposite sides are parallel.

Pentagon: A 2D shape with five angles.

Per: A Latin word meaning 'for each'. We see it in words like per cent (for each hundred).

Per cent: A number followed by the % symbol means the number is divided by 100. It is a way of writing a fraction.

Perimeter: The size of the boundary of a flat object. It is the distance once around it. In Greek *peri* means 'around' and *metria* means 'measurement'.

Periphery: Another word for circumference.

Perpendicular: Two lines which meet or cross at right angles are called perpendicular.

Pi: The number of times bigger the circumference of a circle is than the diameter. It is given a special name because it cannot be written down precisely as a fraction or as a decimal. It is approximately $22/7$ or 3.14159265....

Polyhedron: A general word for an entirely straight-edged 3D shape.

Prism: A 3D shape made by building a 2D shape up from the paper so that it gains thickness, keeping the size and shape of the 2D shape the same. A rod is a prism made by pulling a disc into a 3D shape.

Proportion: A comparative share in something.

Protractor: A circular or semicircular instrument for measuring angles.

Quadrilateral: An entirely straight-sided 2D shape with only four corners.

Radius: The distance from the centre of a circle to its boundary. It is half the diameter. In Latin *radius* means a 'ray' or 'wheel spoke'.

Ratio: A method of comparing different numbers by placing them on either side of a colon (:); for example 1:2. The numbers must be measured in the same units. The order of the numbers matters. A ratio is like a fraction.

Ray: A straight line that starts from a point and goes straight on for ever in one direction only.

Rectangle: A four-sided shape in which pairs of opposite sides are the same length and all four corners are right angles.

Reflection: A 'mirror image' of a shape.

Regular: A regular 2D shape must have all its sides the same length and all its angles the same size.

Rhombus: A four-sided shape with two pairs of parallel sides and all four sides the same length.

Right angle: An angle which is exactly a quarter of a complete turn.

Rod: A solid cylinder which has a length much greater than its diameter.

Rotation: Another word for turn.

Scale: A set of marks on a line used for measuring.

Sector: A piece of a circle, like a piece of a pie.

Semicircle: Half a circle. In Latin *semi* means 'half'.

Set: A collection of things we are interested in.

Single-digit number: A number between 0 and 9.

Slope: A surface or line which is not level. How much (or steeply) it goes up is measured by the ratio UP:ACROSS.

Solid: A 3D object that is completely filled in, i.e. not hollow.

Sphere: A 3D shape made by spinning a circle around a diameter. It may be solid or just a surface.

Square: A regular rectangle with all four sides the same length and four angles of equal size.

Straight angle: An angle that is exactly half a turn.

Surface: The outside of an object.

Symbol: A mark written on paper or something else to stand for a letter, a number or an idea of any kind.

Symmetry: The property of a shape that allows it to be turned about a point or flipped over a line and still look just the same.

Tessellate: To make a perfectly interlocking pattern (from the Latin word *tessella*, meaning 'a small stone used to make mosaic decorations').

Tetrahedron: A 3D shape with four faces, all triangles (from the Greek *tetra*, meaning 'four').

Three-digit number: A number between 100 and 999.

Three-dimensional (3D): A three-dimensional shape (3D) has length and breadth and thickness (depth). It can be solid, just a surface, or even an open framework, like a pylon.

Trapezium: A four-sided 2D shape with one pair of parallel sides.

Triangle: A straight-sided 2D shape with only three corners.

Turn: Another word for angle. A quarter of a turn is 90°, a half turn is 180°, a full turn is 360°.

Turning symmetry: When a pinpoint is pushed through the centre of the shape, it can be turned (less than a complete turn) so that it looks just the same.

Two-dimensional (2D): A two-dimensional shape (2D) has length and breadth but no thickness. Drawings on paper are 2D.

Unit cube: A cube whose sides are one unit (metre, foot, mile etc.) long. Its volume is one cubic unit.

Unit square: A square whose sides are one unit (metre, foot, mile etc.) long. Its area is one square unit.

Units: A word used with measurement. For example, metric units.

Vertex: A point at which two lines cross or meet. Also a point at which three or more edges meet. *See* Corner.

Vertical: Upright, perpendicular to the horizontal.

Volume: The size of a 3D shape. It is measured in cubic units (such as cm^3 or in^3) by counting how many unit cubes can be fitted into it. *See* Capacity.

Index

acute angle 9, 18
angles 6–11, 44
apex 41
arc 38
boundary 38
circles 38, 39
circumference 38
cones 40, 42, 43
cubes 40, 41
cylinders 40, 42, 43
darts 31, 33
designs 40, 41, 42
diagonal 30, 31
diameter 38
disc 42, 43
equilateral triangle 12, 13, 14, 18, 19, 21, 23, 41
flip symmetry 22, 23, 24, 25, 26, 27
geometry symbols 44
hexagon 12, 13, 43
inside angle 6, 15
isosceles triangle 18, 19, 32
kites 31, 33
line of symmetry 22
many-fold symmetry 24–25
nets 40 – *see* designs
obtuse angle 9, 18
octagon 12, 13
ovals 38, 39
parallelograms 15, 31, 34–35

pentagon 12, 13, 43
perpendicular lines 9, 16, 17
polyhedron 41
pyramids 41
quadrilaterals 13, 30–31
radius 38
ray 9
rectangles 25, 31, 36–37
reflection 22, 23
regular shapes 12–13
rhombus 31, 35
right angle 8, 9, 18, 44
right-angled triangles 16–17, 18, 21
rods 40, 42, 43
sectors 39
solid shapes 40–43
spheres 40, 43
squares 12, 13, 15, 24, 31, 37
straight angle 9, 10
symmetry 22–27
tessellating shapes 28–29
tetrahedron 41
three-dimensional (3D) shapes 4, 40, 41, 43
trapeziums 31, 32–33
triangles 14–19, 22–23, 28, 29, 32, 39
turning symmetry 23, 24–25, 26, 27
two-dimensional (2D) shapes 4, 12–39
vertex 7, 41